WORKING-CLASS WIVES

Their Health and Conditions

Margery Spring Rice

Photographs by *Edith Tudor-Hart*

SECOND EDITION

Foreword by *Cecil Robertson*

Introduction by
Barbara Wootton

Virago

Published by VIRAGO Limited 1981
41 William IV Street, London WC2N 4DB

First published by Penguin Books 1939

Copyright © Charles Garrett-Jones,

Ronald Garrett-Jones & Cecil Robertson 1939

Foreword and Notes Copyright © Cecil Robertson 1981

Introduction Copyright © Barbara Wootton 1981

British Library Cataloguing in Publication Data
Spring-Rice, Margery
  Working-class wives.
  1. Women—Great Britain—Social conditions
  2. Women—Great Britain—History—20th century
  3. Labor and laboring classes—
  Great Britain—History—20th century
  I. Title
  305.4′0941   HN49.W6

ISBN 0-86068-153-X

Printed in Great Britain by
The Anchor Press, Tiptree, Essex

CONTENTS

THE WOMEN'S HEALTH ENQUIRY COMMITTEE

Chairman;

Miss Gertrude Tuckwell,
C.H., J.P.,

Mrs. Barton, J.P.
Women's Co-operative Guild.

Mrs. Adrian Corbett,
National Union of Towns-women's Guilds.

Mrs. Neville Dixey
Women's National Liberal Federation.

Mrs. Ayrton Gould, J.P.,[1]
Standing Joint Committee of Industrial Women's Organisations.

Miss Valerie Graham,
Midwives' Institute.

Mrs. E. M. Hubback, M.A., J.P.
National Council for Equal Citizenship.

Mrs. Margaret Rorke, M.B., Ch.B.

Miss Amy Sayle, M.B.E., M.A., L.C.C.
Women Public Health Officers' Association.

Mrs. Wheatcroft, B.A.
Council of Scientific Management in the Home, (National Council of Women).

Mrs. M. L. Spring Rice, M.A. (Hon. Sec.)
N. Kensington Women's Welfare Centre.

The Committee were responsible for the collection of the material upon which this book is based. The book however has been written by one member of the Committee—Mrs. Spring Rice—and no other member is necessarily pledged to all the opinions expressed in the book.

[1] Mrs. Ayrton Gould succeeded Miss Mary Sutherland as the representative of the S.J.C.I.W.O., on the Committee. Owing to increasing pressure of work Mrs. Ayrton Gould was unable to attend the later meetings of the Committee. She therefore resigned before the final recommendations were made.

FOREWORD TO SECOND EDITION

By Cecil Robertson

Margery Spring Rice (my mother) was widely involved in social and political reform, but made no claim to be a specialist. She was passionately concerned about poverty, ill-health and ignorance, and wrote this book to bring some of the reality before other laymen.

In 1980, poverty is certainly less dire and less widespread than it was on the eve of the Second World War. Conditions which have made it more possible for mothers to earn have helped to reduce poverty and to mitigate their terrifying isolation in the home, the National Health Service has made free medical advice accessible to all, and education and the media have made inroads upon ignorance. But working-class mothers of young families are still amongst those hit hardest by bad economic conditions, and it seems to me very important that the category of reader for whom the book was originally intended should find it intelligible. Notes have been added to this edition (p. vii) to put some of the facts and figures into context, and I ask any social historian into whose hands the book falls to make due allowance for my own lack of specialised knowledge.

My thanks are due to Mrs. Freda Parker, of the Family Planning Association's Education Unit, and to David Newbery, of Churchill College, Cambridge, for their help and advice; and to my own family for encouragement, comment and proof-reading.

Cambridge, 1979

INTRODUCTION TO SECOND EDITION

By Barbara Wootton

Forty years ago this book stripped off the veil of indifference and ignorance which concealed the hardships of millions of women from their more prosperous sisters. It is not claimed that the 1,250 working-class wives whose responses to a questionnaire provided the original data would today be regarded as a scientifically selected sample; but there is no reason to suspect that the resulting catalogue of poverty and deprivation was due to any selective bias towards the exceptionally poor or unfortunate.

The reprint of these chronicles is indeed timely. Social historians will value them as documenting large areas of British life on which such detailed personal evidence is seldom available. Contemporary social reformers will reflect whether this book merely portrays the Dark Ages from which we have now happily emerged, or whether forty years on our descendants will be equally shocked by a corresponding chronicle of a working woman's life today.

Throughout the whole of the present century, Britain has fluctuated between dread of over-population, and anxiety that declining birth and death rates would result in a shrinking population heavily over-weighted with the elderly. When this book first appeared, we were in the throes of one of the latter phases. Yet the reader will be struck by the high fertility of the contributors. The two- or three-child family seems to have been quite exceptional, six or seven or even more being much commoner, and in one case 20 is recorded. It must, however, be remembered that in those days contraceptive advice and help was not nearly as accessible as it is today. Even where such help was available, embarrassment and lack of information as to where to go for it would have been formidable obstacles to many women.

Equally remarkable is the melancholy repetition of miscarriages, still-births and deaths in childhood. It seems that several pregnancies were commonly required to produce one child who would survive to maturity. But in this context it should be recalled that out of every thousand babies born alive in England and Wales in 1939, 50·6 were dead before they were a year old, whereas in 1977 the corresponding figure had dropped to below 14; and comparable reductions have also been achieved throughout the years of early childhood.

Much credit for these improvements must of course be given to the work of Infant Welfare Centres, Health Visitors and District Nurses during and after the war. But how many of us realise today that in 1939 a married woman had no access to free medical attention unless she was either expecting, or had recently given birth to, a baby? Her wage-earning husband (unless exceptionally well-paid) would have had the right to the services of a "panel doctor" under the National Insurance Acts, but this did not extend to his wife. Women in fact were treated as merely breeding machines. If they wanted medical attention in their own right, they had to pay for it themselves. So, in the words of one of them, a woman would not "start a doctor's bill if she could possibly stand on her feet".

Not surprisingly, health standards were extremely low. Excessive child-bearing combined with inadequate diets and incessant domestic toil not infrequently produced serious medical conditions which were often left unattended, while constipation and headaches were the standard afflictions of those who escaped more serious illnesses.

Today it is not so certain that fear of the cost is the primary cause (though to judge by the way things are going this may soon regain priority) of working-class women's reluctance to go to the doctor. Medical practitioners are held in awe (and the profession shows no eagerness to abjure this) with the result that potential patients are inhibited by nervousness, which, if they do pluck up courage to enter the surgery, impairs communication; and even more widespread is the dread of the impersonality of hospitals. But the greatest deterrent of all to any mother against seeking medical help is her worry over what will happen to the family if she gives in to illness. In many cases in this book doctors have advised such women to "rest more", or to "stay in bed" and to this day it is not unknown for equally impracticable advice to be handed out to patients in similar circumstances.

I think, however, that we can now confidently say that the average working-class wife eats much better and has better health than the respondents to this survey. But even if it is today exceptional for women to subsist on a diet in which bread and butter and tea are the staple components, cold seems to have replaced malnutrition as the most desperate cause of distress, as the Supplementary Benefits Commission's Reports repeatedly bear witness. Hypothermia may only infrequently appear on certificates as the actual cause of death, but later evidence confirms the finding of the Royal College of Physicians' 1966 Survey that "hypothermia in hospital admissions is common" and that this condition, "whether in association with extensive disease or as a sole clinical sign, is of grave import". Presumably, however, this particular problem chiefly concerns the elderly and the very young. The wives and mothers who (as constantly reported in this book) are "on their feet all day" are perhaps kept reasonably warm by the incessant activity demanded of them.

Perhaps the biggest revolution in the lives of typical wives and mothers which has occurred in the past forty years has been the vast increase in the proportion of them who now take paid employment outside the home. When this book first appeared, hardly any of the respondents had this additional responsibility, and many of their husbands would have regarded it as an insult to their own manliness for their wives to go out to work. Today, however, the child who is said to have summed up the roles of the sexes as "Mummies stay at home, clean the house and get the meals, while daddies go to work and get tired" is out of date – and for pretty well all social classes. By 1971 the employment rate for our married women, which had been rising rapidly in the preceding decade, had reached over 42 per cent, and husbands have learned to swallow their pride in thankfulness for the addition to the family income.

This revolution has at least released women from total captivity in the home. The limitation of social contacts, the deadly monotony, the absence of any defined break between work and leisure consequent upon the woman's home being also her workshop – all these afflictions have been insufficiently recognised by those who do not suffer from them, particularly by the husbands who "go to work and get tired". But the price of escape from this captivity is of course the imposition of a double burden which bears most heavily upon those with children under school age. Labour-saving devices help, and acceptance of a fairer sharing of domestic tasks grows gradually, but there is much to do yet in the modernisation of housing, and in relief of the poverty which mabes some women's employment outside the home a matter not of free choice but of economic necessity

Yet when the final balance is struck, how many of today's manual workers' wives look with envy on their grandmothers' experiences as reflected in this book, and would wish to change places with them?

House of Lords, London 1979

NOTES TO SECOND EDITION

By Cecil Robertson

Medical Services before the National Health Service

DURING the first quarter of the twentieth century, activities in the field of health and welfare were based largely on the Victorian Poor Laws, with their disastrous connotation of destitution and the workhouse; apart from the Poor Laws, the field was covered by voluntary organisations, and it was mainly through these that social reformers of the period aimed to build up both general and specialised services.

The Voluntary Hospitals (dating from the eighteenth century) existed as a result of financial support available locally, rather than as a result of the immediacy of need. Patients paid what they could, which meant that consultants – who were not salaried (this applied also to general practitioners) – were dependent for their livelihood on their more affluent patients, with the inevitable result that in the poorer districts, where need was greatest, facilities were least adequate. Moreover, pressure on beds since the 1860s had been such that these hospitals could cover only emergencies, while the infectious, the chronically sick and incurable, the mentally ill and the old and infirm were relegated to the much lower standards of the hospitals administered by the Poor Law Guardians.

In 1905-9, a Royal Commission examined the situation, but this produced a radical minority report (by Beatrice Webb and other strong-minded persons) condemning the Poor Laws; the majority of the Commissioners disagreed, with the result that little was done. The first real step towards a welfare service based on common citizenship and a positive approach to social problems was the 1911 Health Insurance Act, under which manual workers and those earning not more than £160 a year contributed towards unemployment and sickness benefits. This entitled them to the services of a panel doctor and to free medicines, though not to hospital treatment, nor to any help for dependants other than a maternity grant of 30 shillings. The Act was administered by the Friendly Societies, who could sometimes give additional financial help. The recommendations of a Royal Commission in 1926 that the Act should be extended to cover dependants, and also the care of teeth and eyes, could not be implemented in the economic situation of the time; but nevertheless it was gradually extended, and by the outbreak of war in 1939 approximately half the population was covered, and the upper income limit had been raised to £420 a year.

Up to 1929, nearly all births took place in the home, with or without a midwife in attendance. Successive acts between 1902 and 1936 raised the standards and qualifications required of Midwives, Nurses and Health Visitors, and the Maternity and Child Welfare Act of 1918 started a movement towards the Local Authorities' responsibility for care in this field. The Poor Law (Consolidation) Act of 1927 and the Local Government Act of 1929 gave the County Councils and the County Boroughs the power – though not the obligation – to provide assistance in all lawful ways other than by Poor Relief, and from this point maternity and child welfare came under their wing, and they took over the administration of the old Poor Law hospitals; more maternity beds became available, and by 1936 about a quarter of births were taking place in hospital and the proportion was rising. In 1936, too, the Public Health Act and the Midwives Act consolidated the position, and Local Authorities could provide clinics, home visiting and midwives (salaried), as well as maternity and convalescent homes. However, the discretionary nature of the Local Authorities' brief meant that it was very differently implemented in different areas; the LCC (London County Council), for example, set up a splendid network of municipal hospitals at this time, and Birmingham was notable for excellent clinics and home-help services.

By the beginning of the war, municipal clinics existed on a sufficient scale for about three-quarters of expectant mothers in London to attend them and about three-fifths in other towns, though less than one-fifth elsewhere. For a working-class woman living in the country, the time and cost involved in getting to a town were prohibitive, and she would be entirely dependent on her Health Visitor or District Nurse – which, of course, could be an ideal relationship. Post-natal services in towns were much less adequate, but there were more than 3,000 Local Authority or Voluntary Infant Welfare Centres, covering about 60 per cent of the under-fives. Children of school age came under the care of the school medical inspector.

It will be seen, therefore, that immediately before the war almost everyone had access to some medical services except women who were not actually in process of producing a child and who were too poor to pay doctors' fees.

In 1942, the Beveridge Report on Social Insurance and Allied Services (a best-seller) led to the passing of the 1946 Bill to establish a National Health Service, and in 1948 the Service came into operation, approximately as we know it now.

Prices, wages and the value of money

The shopping list of Mrs B. of Blackburn, given on p. 171 at 8s 11½d (excluding the vanished bars of imperial soap) cost £8.10p in a mainly middle-class supermarket in November 1979 – a multiplying factor of over 18. This is distorted, however, by the fact that the list would doubtless have been different had prices not risen in different degrees – prunes and cocoa, for example, are now luxuries; also, the pre-war 'corner shop' in a poor district would have to keep prices to the barest minimum. Government statistical sources for the same period give the multiplying factor for food at about 13, and for all retail prices at about 15 (the cost of food rose less steeply than other commodities during the war and for 20 years or more afterwards; it is now rapidly catching up).

By and large, it seems that the 1938 pound is around the 6p mark by 1980 values – a multiplying factor of 16/17, but in the same period the wages of manual workers have risen by more than 28 times, so that poverty ought to be on the decline. If it is, the fact that a tenth of Britain's population receives Supplementary Benefits at the time of writing can only lead to the deduction that the case-histories in this book were typical of a very large section of the country indeed.

The Peckham Health Experiment

A Pioneer Health Centre was opened in Peckham in 1926, for families living within one mile of the Centre. It aimed to cater for the physical, mental and social needs of its members, on the grounds that these conditions existed side by side, and to investigate in what good health consisted. The majority of members' incomes turned out to lie between £3 10s and £5 a week, which showed it to be, though unselected, a typical section of urban population.

Regular health checks showed up a large number of latent and unrecognised disorders, particularly in the women; as one example, iron deficiency – which up to the age of 10 was higher in males than in females, was far worse in women of child-bearing age. It also became abundantly clear that the social isolation of women with small children was having a disastrous effect on both health and morale.

The Pioneer Centre closed down in 1928, and its moving spirits, Drs Innes H. Pearce and G. Scott Williamson, produced their report *The Case for Action* in 1931. In 1935 the new Health Centre was opened, and flourished until it was forced to close by the war. By 1936 over 500 families (1,300 individuals) had been medically overhauled, and nearly 80 per cent of these had continued membership under a family subscription. Attempts to revive the Centre after the war failed, no doubt as a result of the inauguration of the National Health Service.

Contraception

The first birth control clinic in England was opened in London by Marie Stopes in 1921, the North Kensington Women's Welfare Centre (of which Margery Spring Rice was a co-founder) in 1924, and in 1930 the National Birth Control Council (which in 1939 became the Family Planning Association) was formed. These were the voluntary, pioneering bodies, and during the later twenties and the thirties other voluntary clinics grew up in increasing numbers. After the 1929 Local Government Act, some authorities opened municipal clinics or made contraceptive advice available in hospitals or in maternity and child welfare clinics.

During the period 1910–19, approximately one-third of Social Class III women at risk used some form of birth control, but only one couple in 20 used any appliance (which would normally have been a condom); by 1935–9 these figures had become one-half and one in four respectively. Non-appliance methods had reached a peak in this social category in the early twenties, declining thereafter as appliance methods increased. Amongst Social Class I women at risk, the increase in the use of appliances came sooner and faster. Appliances recommended by clinics were for the most part caps plus chemicals.

It would seem, therefore, that when respondents in this book quote a doctor or nurse as advising less child-bearing, for at least three-quarters of them – if they heeded the advice at all – what was on offer was abstinence or coitus interruptus, either of which demanded maximum co-operation on the part of husbands.

Births, maternal and child mortality; England and Wales, 1939 and 1977

	1939	1977
Live births per 1,000 population	14·8	11·6
(the peak had been reached in 1947 with a rate of 20·5)		
Still births per 1,000 live births	38	9
Deaths under 1 year per 1,000 live births	50·6	13·8
(this rate stood at 159 in 1900)		
Maternal mortality per 1,000 live births,	3·25	0·13
Deaths under 5 years per 1,000 population: males	16·1	3·4
females	12·7	2·7

A Ministry of Health investigation during 1932–7 had failed to establish any positive correlation between maternal mortality and social class, overcrowding or unemployment, in spite of enormous variations between the rates in different areas; for example, in the Rhondda Valley between January 1935 and July 1937, the puerperal death rate of a large sample was 1·64, compared with 6·15 over another large sample elsewhere in Wales, and the corresponding still-birth and neo-natal rates were about half. A substantial proportion of maternal deaths were recorded as following abortion (about 15 per cent) and doubtless there were many others not so recorded, following attempted abortion.

During the thirties, of deaths occurring during the first month of life, about 70 per cent were due to prematurity or to conditions present at birth. Of those who died between one month and one year of age, 23 per cent were still due to these causes and 52 per cent to diarrhoea and infectious diseases. For children between one and five, measles and pneumonia (plus whooping cough for girls) were the main killers, followed by diphtheria, and for children of school age diphtheria was the chief cause, closely followed by accidents in the case of the boys. In early adult life tuberculosis headed the list, and 15 per cent of deaths throughout the population were due to tuberculosis and other infectious diseases.

School meals and milk

From 1906, the education service had been bound to provide a midday meal for children whose education might otherwise suffer; this was not to be classed as Poor Relief, and parents were expected to contribute if they could. By 1939, about 12 per cent of the school population was eating a school meal, and about a quarter were taking milk. These figures stood at around 70 per cent and 95 per cent respectively in the mid-seventies, but are now lower owing to escalating meal prices and alterations in eligibility for free milk.

References

Documents on Health and Social Services 1834 to the Present Day, Brian Watkin, (Methuen)

A Social History of Medicine, F. F. Cartwright, (Longman)

Why the Poor Pay More, ed. Frances Williams, (National Consumer Council)

Report on British Health Services 1937, (PEP)

The National Health Service – the First Thirty Years, (HMSO)

CSO Annual abstract of Statistics 1952 and 1979, (HMSO)

Royal Commission on Population 1949, (HMSO)

INTRODUCTION

By Dame Janet Campbell

No one who has ever taken part in Maternity and Child Welfare work can have failed to become interested in the well-being of the mother after she has passed outside the scope of the organisation which has grown up as a result of endeavours to protect infancy and motherhood.

Work for infant welfare had its origin in the shocked recognition of the wholly unnecessary sacrifice of infant life and health as shown by the high rates of infant mortality which existed in the early years of the present century. The reduction of this death rate by more than 50%, and the higher standard of health which we now find among surviving infants are due in great measure to the education of Mothers in better methods of mothercraft through the influence of the Infant Welfare Centre and the health visitor, as well as to a general desire to secure a healthier environment for little children, and a wider understanding of their needs and requirements.

Inquiry into the causes of infant mortality soon made it clear that the health of the child before and after birth was intimately bound up with the health of the mother herself, and that prevention of avoidable death and injury associated with child bearing would save infant life as well as reduce the physical and mental suffering associated with maternity. The reduction of maternal mortality and morbidity is a far more difficult and complex problem than the establishment of better health among infants, but there are welcome signs that this, too, is yielding to the patient and persistent co-operative effort of those concerned with professional practice and public health administration.

A series of Acts of Parliament, such as the Notification

of Births Acts (1907 and 1915), The Maternity and Child Welfare Act (1918), and the successive Midwives Acts (1902–1936) give wide powers to Local Authorities which are being extensively used for the benefit of the pregnant and nursing mother and the child under five years of age. When the child is old enough to go to school he comes under the protection of the School Medical Service with its medical and nursing supervision, and treatment of certain disabling ailments and defects; he also has the advantages of school meals and milk, physical education, special schools and so forth; eventually he comes under the National Health Insurance Act.

The mother, on the other hand, remains within the purview of the official organisation only so long as she is a "nursing mother", that is, in general terms, until her child is one year old. After that, unless and until she again becomes pregnant, she is not eligible for advice, treatment or social assistance under the Maternity and Child Welfare Act, and unless she is an employed insured woman, which the majority of married women are not, the State is not officially concerned with her physical condition or with the provision of any remedies which may possibly be needed.

The health and happiness of the working married woman are clearly of great importance in considering national health as a whole. She has to bear a heavy burden of physical work and mental responsibility. On her depends very largely the success or otherwise of the family life of the greater part of our population. Comparatively few people realise the long hours of monotonous unrelieved domestic drudgery needed to keep her home and surroundings clean and wholesome, to buy and prepare food, and to attend to the manifold wants of her husband and children in sickness and health. Fewer still appreciate fully the effects on a woman's health and mental outlook of the incessant struggle needed to stretch an inadequate income to its utmost limits, and of her restricted environment and the scanty opportunities for recreation or social intercourse during the small amount of leisure she is able to snatch from her daily toil. It is often heartbreaking to see how rapidly a pretty attractive girl grows old and drab after a few years of marriage. She loses her looks and ceases to take a pride in her appearance; minor ailments are neglected, her temper is frayed, and household worries weigh unnecessarily heavy. Improved housing conditions, where they exist, have to some extent lightened the load of domestic duty, have brought greater comfort and a little more elbow room; but even so the needs of the husband and children are inevitably the first consideration and the mother has seldom anyone to notice her fatigue or her ailments, to advise her in domestic or family difficulties, or to show her how to bring brightness and variety into her daily routine. People who lightly censure the woman gossiping on her doorstep, untidy and even slatternly as she may seem, often fail to realise how completely she is tied to her own small home, and how few opportunities she has of escaping from the wear and tear of family life at close quarters. The cinema has done something to bring mental peace and refreshment, but it costs more money than she can often afford; wireless is beyond the means of many homes. The success of the Infant Welfare Centre is in some degree attributable to the pleasure the mother finds in spending an afternoon away from home and in meeting kindly doctors and nurses as well as other women with whom she can talk.

If the well-grown girl we see leaving school is to preserve her physical fitness into middle and old age something must be done to watch over her health and to give her interests and recreation which she can never find unaided for herself. At the same time there is an imperative obligation upon our social system to do more to relieve and rationalise the domestic slavery under which many women live (for it is nothing less), by offering better municipal or communal services to the housewife, and by educating at least the younger women to make intelligent use of them.

The standard of health of the average working woman is usually far below what it might be. The experience of the ante- and post-natal clinic has given us some insight into the state of her general health as well as a growing knowledge of the ailments and injuries which may be associated with pregnancy and childbirth. We find that the expectant mother is often mal-nourished; she is frequently anæmic; indigestion and constipation are accepted as a matter of course; varicose veins and dental caries pass almost unnoted except perhaps when pregnancy accentuates the aching and weariness of her legs, or causes a more rapid decay of defective teeth.

The more careful the post-natal supervision the larger the number of minor injuries or misplacements which are discovered, apart from any serious damage which may require immediate attention. Unfortunately, it is a much more difficult task to persuade a mother to seek or accept post-natal advice for herself than to induce her to ask for guidance in infant management. Many women still get no adequate post-natal care at all once the midwife has finished her duties; many others continue to postpone treatment which is advised until they drift beyond the care of the maternity organisation, and the matter is permanently disregarded to the detriment, greater or less, of subsequent health and vitality.

Meanwhile the anæmia and dyspepsia continue, and the woman frequently suffers from various aches and pains which may not incapacitate her, but which do reduce her physical vigour and energy and make her increasingly dispirited and irritable. It is relatively easy to obtain excellent treatment for an acute or serious illness either at a voluntary or municipal hospital, but minor sickness is apt to be ignored partly because there is no easy remedy. The hospital out-patient department is too busy and crowded for interest to be taken in small common disorders; the panel doctor, even if available, is also too busy to go much beyond the bottle of medicine or other placebo. There is no medical adviser sufficiently concerned with the woman's general health and mental hygiene, apart from immediate symptoms, to find time to listen patiently to her troubles, and not only to prescribe pills or medicine but to give the careful and individual advice needed by a particular woman, or to take note of conditions which may be danger signals pointing to the early stages of serious diseases.

And apart from medical care, both the younger and the middle-aged women need amusement, exercise and recreation; they need somewhere, near at home, to spend what leisure they have, and they need teaching how to use that leisure and how to make the most of it. They need encouraging to feel a wholesome impatience with remediable discomforts and trials, and some stimulating influence to counteract the inevitable apathy which so naturally settles upon them, as well as practical assistance to rid themselves of some of the almost intolerable weight of unpaid domestic labour which presses so hardly, and which is spoiling not only their own lives but the contribution to national health and efficiency which they might make as happy wives and mothers.

It is one thing, however, to be certain in one's own mind that this problem of ill-health exists, and quite another to prove it statistically or to measure its magnitude with any exactness. Precise data could only be obtained by painstaking and continued medical observation of large numbers of women over long periods, and this is unhappily impracticable. Records of sickness among insured women may be suggestive, but are not sufficiently complete, or indeed of the type, to be of real use. The invaluable scientific work being done by Dr. Williamson and Dr. Innes Pearce at the Pioneer Health Centre in Peckham deals with only a small section of women in London. Yet it is difficult to arouse general interest in a new social problem when there are already so many pressing and well-established causes claiming attention, or to create the sympathy necessary to find the means of dealing with it, unless some proof of its existence and of its urgency can be brought forward to convince public opinion.

That is what the Women's Health Enquiry Committee have endeavoured to do, in perhaps the only way possible in present circumstances. They do not claim that the evidence collected provides sufficient material for a statistical report, but only that it is a careful and true sample of the conditions under which a very large section of the community would be found to be living were a wider survey undertaken. The stories upon which this book is based have been gathered from different parts of the country and are completely unedited. They describe in the words of the women themselves, most poignantly and movingly, the life which is the lot of many; and they reveal plainly the claims which these patient, courageous, inarticulate mothers might well make to a greater share in the benefits which medical services, public health administration, and facilities for physical education are bringing to the community as a whole.

It was the wisdom and foresight of unofficial pioneer workers which led the way to our Maternity and Child Welfare Service; it seems fitting and proper that the voluntary effort of women deeply concerned to bring greater happiness to other women less fortunate than themselves should point out this gap in our social services, and should contribute many practical suggestions for the remedy of ills which, once recognised, we must all deplore and desire to remove.

WORKING-CLASS WIVES

CHAPTER I

THE MOTHER IN THE FAMILY GROUP

THE family is Nature's first group. It is biologically indispensable. In spite of the disintegrating influences of civilisation, it is still within the family that individual character and physical health are mainly formed; and that the strongest affections are focussed.

Organised societies have all recognised the primary necessity of this group, but yet have tended to break in upon and to break up its separateness. They have done this in order to use the individual human being in the interests of the community system and, to some extent, by pooling and directing his labour, they have returned to him and to his family a larger share of greater benefits, material, intellectual and cultural, than he could have got for himself if he had remained the direct producer of the simple necessities of life for those dependent upon him. Every modern economic system tries to organise the labour of the recognised producer in any family so that, in co-operation with other brains and hands, it can produce most. This has an important bearing not only on the material welfare of the family as a whole, but on the mind and habits of each member. The very large majority of men (who are the recognised producers-in-chief) work away from their homes and return there for rest and recreation. In nearly all families all children except the very youngest spend a great deal of time away from home, either in school, or, if they have left school, in their own wage-earning jobs. For them too the home is a place for play or rest.

For fathers and children alike these hours away from home bring new contacts, recreational, such as clubs, camps and games, as well as more serious interests. But in general the mother stays at home.

This abiding maternal personality plays a large part in the stubborn persistence of the family tradition. Although, with the increasing opportunities and complexities of social organisation, the activities and interests of the other members of the family tend to multiply, the magic of the hearth remains unchallenged. Undoubtedly it is rooted deep in all human nature, but the mother is the human anchor which holds it fast.

For most women this is no pedestal of ease and mere moral power, for in the large majority of homes the woman is not only the most passionate upholder of the faith, but the slave without whose labour the whole structure of the family tends to collapse. To whatever social class she belongs, the health and happiness of her husband and children are her most sacred responsibility; but it is only a very small number of women who are able to buy comparative freedom from the actual work which this involves. The emancipation for which many thousand women have worked in the last hundred years, has had little or no effect on the domestic slavery of mind and body of the millions with whom rests the immediate care of a home and family. Indeed a curious phenomenon in the position of women is that those who most need some measure of freedom from the restrictions of family duties, are often the first to resist the legislation which might give it to them. They are passionately jealous of any usurpation or delegation of their own authority.[1]

---

[1] Examples of this are provided in the great difficulty which occurs in persuading women to go into hospital for their confinements. Although trained home helps can be provided to look after the father and children the mother shows an inherent disinclination to entrust her home even temporarily to the care of someone else. Again, mothers themselves have often been the first to oppose the granting of school meals for their children, holding that it is unnatural for the children to eat away from home and that they prefer to prepare the food

It is, however, not only their own inertia and prejudice which hold these women enslaved by their domestic duties. It would be logical to suppose that the work of caring for the home and family, which is the most fundamental of all human activity, would be the first to profit by modern methods of socialisation and scientific management. But the rationalisation of labour has passed over the working mother, leaving her to carry on in more or less the same primitive way that has been customary since the world began; never specialising and seldom learning real skill in any of her dozens of different jobs.

These features of the problem apply very largely to all countries, with the exception of Russia where the socialisation of labour has included domestic work, giving the woman freedom to work outside her home; and U.S.A. where even the poorest woman demands, and can generally get, labour-saving devices hardly dreamt of even in middle-class English homes. But there is a further obstacle to the solution of the problem which belongs to this country alone. In England, side by side with the passionate wish to preserve the integrity of the family, there is found the determination to keep it as a whole as *separate* as possible from other families and from any outside intrusion. There was for a long time in this country an inherent dislike of flats amongst rich and poor alike, because to share a staircase or lift with another family, to have another family living overhead or underneath, was considered a violation of that privacy which is the family's inalienable right.[1]

---

themselves. Another example is the opposition from many parents with which the Ministry of Labour was met in the initial stages of their scheme to remove adolescent wage-earners from the distressed areas. The boys and girls after leaving school are placed in hostels in different parts of the country, with the object of training them for and placing them in jobs which could be found for them more easily in these districts. The Ministry has had to devote much time and propaganda to breaking down the parental prejudice against this "unnatural" disintegration of the family.

[1] In the debates in the House of Commons in February and March 1938 on the Housing (Financial Provisions) Bill, such speakers of

This sort of objection is one with which all housing reformers have constantly to contend, the dislike of sharing amenities such as gardens, washhouses, central heating and restaurants, though consideration of space and economy may make it quite impossible to provide them separately for each house. It is submission to this almost religious faith that causes housing authorities to build small houses instead of blocks of flats, even where the value of land demands the most stringently economical use, and where the ground space saved by building perpendicularly rather than horizontally could be laid out in ornamental gardens, playing grounds, swimming pools, and all sorts of workshops, recreational and domestic, for women as well as for men and children.

This is not a prejudice only of the poor. There is hardly a garden in England which is not surrounded by wall or hedge or railing, the obscurer the better. There is hardly a London Square garden which is not protected from the public by padlock and key. There is hardly a window in any family house which is not curtained effectively to obscure the view of the inquisitive passer-by. And as a consequence there is no play or book or film so successful as that which deals with the intimacies of family life, which, except in *one* family,—his or her own—are a complete mystery to the ordinary man or woman ! The

---

authority and enlightenment as Sir Percy Harris enjoined the Minister of Health, (Sir Kingsley Wood) "not to ignore the instinct of the English family to prefer even a very commonplace old-fashioned house to one of these modern flats in a five-storey building. . . . We do not want our cities to become, as on the Continent, cities of flat-dwellers". Similar opinions were expressed, sometimes in the strongest terms, by many other members; one, Mr. Macquisten, K.C. (member for Argyllshire) going so far as to say that "flats are an abomination . . . never meant for human beings. . . . Flats make Communists while cottages make individuals and,—incidentally make good Conservatives. . . . Any sensible Briton would sooner live in a little wooden shack of his own with a quarter of an acre, than in the finest flat or hotel". See Hansard, February 15th, col. 1758, et seq. and March 3rd, col. 1326 et seq.

causes of the strength of this English tradition would be an interesting study for the sociologist and cannot be pursued here. Perhaps the reason is to be found in the English Channel; we are born and bred as islanders and the sea may be responsible for more than its work of pure ablution !

Be this as it may, this Monroe doctrine for the family has a profound effect on the life of the working-class mother. Not only has she resisted, as has been pointed out, reforms which aim at relieving her of some of her work by handing it over to other persons or authorities, but she has largely obstructed the reforms which, though they would not take away her work, would make it easier by giving her communal amenities. She would share these with other women like herself, and they might be situated outside the four walls of her home; she therefore distrusts them for she believes passionately in "keeping herself to herself".[1]

The inadaptability of our ideas of the sanctity of the family and home may have retarded the provision which wise Governments and reformers seek to make for the prosperity and happiness of the community. It may be that women are largely responsible for the slowness of progress of which they are themselves the victims, but it is certain that their lives are profoundly affected by the rigidity of the tradition, and the object of the following pages is to awaken the public conscience to the urgent need for help, educational as well as practical, for that section of humanity which is in fact the tap-root of our national welfare—the working mothers. Their task is more un-

---

[1] One of the outstanding disadvantages of the large housing estates, e.g. Dagenham, is that by removing families from tenement buildings they have destroyed that compulsory neighbourliness which was a feature of the old system. Women who came from such tenements have been known to object in their new houses to sharing even a front door step with their neighbours. The belief that because each little house had its own square patch of private "garden," public parks or recreation grounds were unnecessary, resulted often in an almost disastrous isolation of each family, and will have to be modified.

remitting than that of any man, and it is only the strongest
of them who are able to keep level with it and to prevent
the tragic slipping back in health, in happiness, and in
cultural if not in moral standards, which is too often seen.
The last thing that can be expected of them is quiet thought
and any action other than the minimum demanded by the
immediate job in hand. They lead private and often very
solitary lives; their work is unpaid and unorganised. Its
inevitability is taken for granted not only by themselves
but also by the other half of the public, who themselves
have grown up and thrived upon it. Members of Parliament for whom now the women can cast their vote, do
not see what is going on in the small dark unorganised
workshop of the home. Men and young people who work
in large communities and in the political limelight of the
factory, the railway or the mine, have time and energy
and opportunity to make their voices heard. And though
the better economic conditions which are the basis of most
of their demands would benefit their wives and families
most of all, there is none the less a primitive acceptance
by the men, as well as by the women themselves, of the
general conditions of a housewife's life.[1] They know that
on the whole the women *like* their work. What this book
aims at pointing out is the stealthy and sinister deterioration of the woman's health and happiness, which it is the
concern of men as well as of women to arrest.

The woman comes onto the map of the public conscience
only when she is performing the bodily function of pro-

---

[1] It was recently reported to the writer by the Agent of a large
estate where the agricultural wage was 33/– that he is unable to persuade
the labourer to do overtime work; because as the district is very remote
and public transport non-existent, the men cannot go easily to a town
for amusement or recreation. They therefore say they have nothing
to spend the extra money on ! It is no indictment of their goodwill or
affection for their families, but evidence only of their blind acceptance
of their home conditions and especially of the sort of lives that their
wives lead, that they do not think of buying her anything which might
lighten her work or brighten her outlook, let alone extra food for the
whole family.

ducing a child, and indeed during the last twenty years (the Maternity and Child Welfare Act was passed in 1918), there has been a spate of scientific investigation and of anxious consideration of her health and welfare as the human casket of the precious unborn life. Because maternal mortality figures have not shown that susceptibility to the progress of medical science and the improvement of maternal services that could be desired, medical opinion is now fully alive to the fact that the function of child birth, although a perfectly natural one, is fraught with danger and requires the highest degree of expert study and care.[1]

Upon the survival of the mother depend the growth and care of the family, and a high rate of maternal mortality threatens in more ways than one the very existence of the race. Dame Janet Campbell wrote in 1924:—"The unexpected loss of the mother is a tragedy to the family. It is not infrequently associated with the death of the infant for whom the maternal life has been sacrificed, and is often followed by the impaired health and nutrition of the remaining children".[2] Moreover, the psychological effect of danger is believed by some experts to be very far-reaching and to account in some measure for the falling birth rate. But, in the absolutely proper concern about the complex problems, medical and social, of this important matter, maternal morbidity, i.e. damage or disease resulting from child birth, has tended to be overlooked. It is not that experts are unaware of its wide-spread incidence, but it is undoubtedly much more difficult to assess morbidity and impossible to collect accurate figures. "The mortality returns reveal only a part of the damage and disability, and an incalculable amount of unreported and often untreated injury and ill-health results from

[1] The rise in total maternal mortality (i.e. including deaths from associated causes) per thousand live births in the ten years, 1923–1933, is from 4.83 to 5.94, a rise of 22%.

[2] Reports on Public Health and Medical Subjects. No. 25, H.M. Stationery Office, 1924, page 5.

pregnancy and labour."[1] The woman can and does escape the vigilance of those institutions and individuals who might look after her when, having borne her child, she returns to normal life. The damage may not be visible to a casual observer or even to the Doctor whom she consults (perhaps) for her baby, either privately or at the Welfare Centre. She is alive, and that is what matters, and in most cases she herself will think it perfectly natural if she has lost a little of her old energy and sense of well-being.

It has seemed to those who are responsible for the investigations of which this book forms a survey, that for an improvement of maternal welfare there are four factors which deserve immediate attention. First of all, maternal *morbidity* is extremely widespread and enduring, so that a woman tends to become progressively less fit with the birth of each child. Secondly, though some of the contributory causes to maternal ill-health date back to childhood or adolescence most of them are found in the conditions of the mother's present environment and work. Thirdly, there is a great deal of ill-health amongst married working-class women which escapes notice and treatment altogether because it is *not* connected with the process of child-bearing, but which none the less seriously impairs efficiency as house-wives and as mothers. And lastly, the married working-class woman is in a category by herself as regards the problems which concern the well-being of her family; not only because of the loneliness, isolation and primitive conditions of her work but also because her heart as well as her brains and hands is engaged in her labour. How far these conclusions are justified by the facts of the case will appear in the following pages.

[1] Dame Janet Campbell, op. cit.

CHAPTER II

AIMS AND METHODS OF THE WOMEN'S HEALTH ENQUIRY COMMITTEE

THE Women's Health Enquiry Committee was formed in 1933 of representatives from certain women's organisations and on an entirely non-political basis. The personnel of the Committee will be found on page vi.

Their aims were to investigate the general conditions of health among women, especially among married working-class women, in view of indications that ill-health was both more widespread and more serious than was generally known

These indications are found in:—

1. The Final Report of the Departmental Committee on Maternal Mortality and Morbidity (1932) which states that difficult confinements and impaired health after child-birth are caused as often by neglected health during early womanhood as by lack of care during pregnancy and parturition, and that ill-health directly resultant from child-birth and insufficient pre-natal and post-natal care is often prolonged after the patient has passed out of the care of the maternity services.
2. The Reports by the Government Actuary (1930 and 1932) showing increases in claims both for sickness and disablement benefit under the National Health Insurance Acts.

As a first step the Committee set out for investigation as far as practicable:—

1. The incidence and nature of general ill-health among working-class women.
2. Its possible causes, such as lack of medical treatment, poverty, bad housing, over-work.

3. How far women observe the ordinary rules of health and hygiene, and the extent to which a certain amount of ill-health is accepted as inevitable.

The Committee decided to undertake only a "sample" enquiry, i.e. to collect information from women in widely differing districts, social conditions and occupations; married and unmarried women: insured and uninsured. The evidence collected would not be sufficient for statistical purposes, but would serve to illustrate what may be expected as the result of a more searching scientific investigation.[1]

Every possible safeguard was taken that the cases, necessarily few in number, from each district, social or economic class, should not in any way be selected from those women who were known to be in bad health. The selection is not entirely random because the women visited were already on the panel of the various organisations whose help was enlisted. The majority of dossiers were collected by city or country Health Visitors, whose panel is formed not from sick women but from the register of recent births. Health Visitors and such other investigators as Women's Co-operative Guild secretaries, University Settlement visitors, factory welfare workers and Salvation Army organisers were asked to take consecutive cases in their daily or weekly visits, omitting only those women who were unwilling to co-operate. It can therefore fairly be claimed that the investigation provides an honest sample of the health and the social and domestic environment of the average working-class mother.

A questionnaire was issued in two parts; Form A contained questions about social conditions, type of house, district, occupation, income, etc. These, being to a certain extent objective questions, could be answered by the

[1] This procedure has a valuable precedent in the volume of letters from working-class women entitled "Maternity" collected and published in 1917 by the Women's Co-operative Guild. This was the first organised attempt to rouse public opinion on conditions of childbirth in working-class homes, and the challenge was taken up by many Women's Organisations and finally by the Ministry of Health.

investigator on data supplied to her by the woman. Form B dealt with health and matters relevant to health only and was designed to provide a precise account by the woman herself of her daily life and condition.

The questions asked were as follows:—

Form A.

1. Name of street and town or village.
2. Type of street or neighbourhood.
3. Type of dwelling.
   (*a*) Whole house or cottage, self-contained flat; rooms.
   (*b*) Has it any drawbacks? If so, what are they?
4. Number of rooms occupied by your family.
5. Number in family.
6. Is there a separate W.C. for your family? If not, by how many is one W.C. used?
7. Is there a separate water supply for your family?
8. How do you get cold water?
9. How do you get hot water?
10. Is there a yard or garden to your house which you can use?
11. What is your husband's occupation?
12. What paid work, if any, do you do outside your home?
13. How much do you have for housekeeping? How much of this goes in rent?
14. Your own age.
15. How long have you been married?
16. How many children have you had.
17. Have you had any miscarriages or still-births? If so, how many?
18. Ages of children living at home. (*a*) Boys. (*b*) Girls.
19. Are you insured under the National Health Insurance Act? Have you a panel doctor?
20. Whom do you consult when you feel ill?
21. What regular payments do you or your husband make to —(*a*) Hospitals? (*b*) Nursing Associations?
22. What treatment have you had in return for these payments?
   (*a*) Hospital: Out Patient.
                    In Patient.
   (*b*) Nursing.

Form B.

1. Do you usually feel fit and well?

2. If not, what do you suffer from ? (Please put each ailment separately below, and answer each of the questions about it separately. Include quite minor ailments, such as constipation, toothache, headache, rheumatism, faintness, etc.)

   Name of Ailment.

   How long have you felt this ?

   What do you think is the cause ?

   Do you take any remedy ? If so, what ?

   Have you had any advice about it from a doctor, nurse, clinic or hospital ? Give details.

3. What was your occupation before marriage ?

4. About how much time did you have off through ill-health during the last 5 years you were working ?

5. What form did your ill-health take ? Give details if possible.

6. (a) When must you get up in the morning ?

   (b) When do you go to bed at night ?

7. How many hours a day are you on your feet ?

8. How much leisure time do you have on an average working day and how do you spend it ?

9. Please write in detail an average day's diet for *yourself*, and stating which food is fresh and which is preserved or tinned.

   Breakfast.

   Dinner.

   Tea.

   Supper.

   How often do you drink tea during the day ?

   How much water do you drink ?

10. How often do you have :—

    (a) eggs, (b) fresh fish, (c) fresh vegetables.

11. What special difficulties are there about your home or housework ?

12. Have you had any teaching about your health and how to keep well ? If so, where and from whom ?

Adequate space was allowed for the answers to these questions, and the women were encouraged to, and often did, give supplementary accounts of their health, on the backs of the forms.

It cannot be claimed that all the answers given are accurate and in no case do the Committee wish to base any statistics on the result of the investigation; but this it is felt does not invalidate the findings which, taken as a whole, combine to give a very fair picture of the sort of life these women lead. A few tables will be found at the end of this book which, although a claim of complete accuracy cannot be made even for them, are nevertheless of value for purposes of comparison; incidentally it is obvious that error when it occurs is more often on the side of understatement than on that of exaggeration.

The Committee hoped to get a large number of question-naires filled in by women of a better economic and social position and by unmarried women of all classes. Such dossiers would have served as "controls" for those of the particular women with whose welfare the Committee were most concerned. But in this they were disappointed. Although a large number of forms were given to factory and shop welfare workers, superintendents of girls clubs, etc., who were willing to co-operate, most of them were returned unanswered. Finally only 60 questionnaires from unmarried women were filled in, and it has not been felt worth while to analyse them for the purpose of inclusion in this book.

The failure to obtain information from middle-class women is more surprising and disappointing. The Committee had to rely almost entirely on personal contact and acquaintance for data from this class, but here again inertia and unwillingness obstructed the collection of more than a very few completed interrogatories. The woman who feels, quite justifiably, that the responsibility for the greater portion of her misfortune is not her own but that of a faulty economic system or of inadequate facilities, is able and willing to ventilate them when given an easy opportunity, and has nothing to lose from publicity. But she who either does not need remedies or who should find them for herself, will not wish to talk about matters which are no one's affair but her own or which would not do credit to her intelligence and initiative.

The data on which the following chapters are based are extracted therefore from the answers made by 1,250 women, all married and all of that section of society in which the whole domestic work is done by the woman herself. A few of them are widows and these in most cases go out to work; a few are old women who may be living with a married son or daughter, but their health record is none the less relevant to the enquiry. A few others also supplement their husbands' wages or unemployment pay by daily or intermittent work outside the home.

Even, therefore, although the Committee cannot supply sufficient "control" figures from unmarried women or from married women in a better economic position, the investigation has produced overwhelming evidence that the conditions of life of the working-class mothers of whom these 1,250 form a sample, are such as to make it impossible to maintain after marriage the standard (often low enough) of health and well-being which was possible to them as unmarried working girls and would be possible to them still if their incomes were fantastically larger. These conditions are examined in the following chapters.

The enquiry, limited though its nature and scope have been, has taken much longer than was at first anticipated. In the first place, a change was made in the questionnaire which entailed a new start a year after the Committee was formed. Secondly, except for the analysis and tabulation of the completed forms, which were entrusted to a trained statistician, the whole of the enquiry has been conducted voluntarily. It was found very early in the work that the people who might easily have given time to visiting were not those best fitted to approach women with such intimate questions; and that for satisfactory results the Committee would have to call upon trained investigators, such as Health Visitors, who were already on terms of intimacy with the women they visited. Such investigators are necessarily extremely busy and the Committee are deeply sensible of the debt they owe to those public workers who had this enquiry superimposed on their every-day routine work and to the Medical Officers of Health who allowed some of the valuable time of their visiting officers to be spent upon it. A further delay was occasioned by the unfortunate illness of the statistical worker who undertook the analysis of the completed forms.

This survey, therefore, instead of coinciding with the initial stages of the Nation's physical fitness campaign, is appearing at a moment when already a great deal of publicity has been given to the need of a better standard of national health and when particular aspects of the subject have already been widely investigated and remedies suggested. Expert Committees have examined and continue to examine problems of nutrition, the essential needs of children, the improvement of recreational facilities, housing, conditions of work, the effects, moral and physical, of unemployment, and last but not least the needs of the mother in pregnancy and child-birth. But curiously little attention is paid, and *no* scientific method is applied to the problems and needs of the woman as housewife, as family chancellor, as friend, companion, nurse to her husband and children, or even as mere human being. It is to be hoped that this book will help to dispel that cruel and dangerous inertia and that remedies will be sought for much of the avoidable unhappiness, loneliness, ugliness and ill-health which are the lot of thousands of working-class wives for a great number of the years of their lives. Here is the soil upon which must be laid the foundations of that finer and stronger national life to which so much courageous effort is now directed. No shattering modifications are needed either in the view of the sanctity of the home, or in the woman's function in family life; on the contrary, when once public imagination has been aroused, it will surely be recognised that the quality of both will be immeasurably raised, to the lasting benefit of every member of the community, when the labour of the house-wife receives the acknowledgment and consideration which it deserves.

CHAPTER III

THE INCIDENCE AND TREATMENT
OF ILL-HEALTH

"The calf destroys the flanks of its mother"
Old Welsh proverb.

A SOMEWHAT arbitrary division into four groups of health
has been made among the 1,250 women whose records
have been collected; the first group is of those in *apparently*
good health, 392 cases (31·3%). These are the women
who say that they feel fit and well, who appear to
have had little or no treatment for any ailment or to
have been cured of previous complaints. Few of them
speak of difficulties or hardships which give indirect evidence
of any condition incompatible with good health.

The second group, 278 cases (22·3%) is of those in
indifferent health. The majority of them have answered
"yes", to the first question ("Do you usually feel fit and
well"), but have then recorded one or more ailments of
a chronic nature which do not justify a classification of
good health. It has not been thought fair to put them
into either of the two bad health groups, though the
chronicle of disorders which follows their first affirmative
answer testifies to their morbidity.

The third group, 190 cases (15·2%) is of those who give
variously modified affirmative answers to the first question,
but whose ailments are so numerous, so serious or so
enduring that the answer "fairly well", "on and off",
etc., to the first enquiry has been taken as a courageous
attempt to make light of their condition. These women
have been classed as having bad health.

The last group, 390 cases (31·2%) is of those whose condition is very grave. They say "No" or "Never" to the

first question and give ample records of serious chronic conditions and often much additional indirect evidence to justify this answer.

Now it must be very clearly remembered throughout the reading of this and the following chapters that this investigation did not involve any medical examination of the women, or any reference to medical reports concerning them, (such as the records kept by Hospitals, Clinics, Insurance doctors, Welfare Centres, etc.). The accounts of their health, circumstances and opinions are given by the women themselves, generally not only in their own words but in their own hand-writing. Sometimes the help of the health visitor or other investigator has been enlisted, and often the visitor herself has added some note to the woman's record, after the form has been completed; but this report invariably distinguishes between such notes and the original account given. A very few forms have been distributed by doctors amongst their working-class patients, but these forms too were completed by the woman herself, without the help of the doctor.

It can be confidently stated that these women, (and it would be true of nearly all women living in similar circumstances) *do not exaggerate their bad health.* On the contrary, bad health almost certainly exists in many dozens of these women who either are not aware of it or do not know from what disease they suffer. Many others deliberately ignore it because they realise that the cure is for them impracticable or involves chimerical changes in the social system, for which they do not dare even to hope; in self-protection therefore it is better to cheat themselves into a stubborn assertion of well-being than to add one more torment to their manifold troubles and responsibilities. Lack of education in the matter and of any opportunity of ever having *formed* a high standard of good health means that even without conscious self-deception the woman has a conception of fitness far inferior to that of the more favoured and prosperous sections of the community. Against the latter the charge of hypochondria can only too often be brought, but there is not the slightest evidence of this throughout these 1,250 personal records of life and health.

It is not going to be argued here that anything less than what might be called an expert standard of good health, (such as was presumably the criterion in the investigation at the Peckham Health Centre, see footnote 1) is incompatible with a vigorous and healthy condition. But a vast gulf stretches between the standard of physical fitness demanded by the medical profession and the mere absence of sickness or disabling disease which is the criterion of good health accepted by the working mother. She firmly believes that her home and family would collapse if her work was interrupted by a sojourn at the hospital, or even by the necessity of lying down or resting in bed for a few hours a day and she therefore refuses to admit that she is ill, until these disastrous interruptions to her

[1] Dr. Scott-Williamson and Dr. Pearce, the medical directors of the Peckham Pioneer Health Centre, have in the course of 18 months medically examined 1,530 individuals (men, women and children) of the families-members of the centre. In only 9% of these has nothing wrong been found, and 83% have something the matter and are doing nothing about it. Of this group, the doctors say that "the majority are unaware that they are less than perfectly healthy. . . . The most exuberant sense of well-being may be associated with most serious disorder. Hence the recognition of well-being as a cloak covering every sort of disorder is of primary importance." It is to be noted that these examinations were amongst people in much better financial circumstances than the majority of the families from whom the 1,250 women of *this* report are taken. If Drs. Pearce and Scott-Williamson had limited their investigation to the *women* (even of such better-circumstanced families), they would in all probability have found the percentage of those with "something the matter" much higher; partly because the deliberate self-deception is more prevalent in the mothers, and partly because the health of school children receives now a great deal of medical care and attention. And the men, *nine-tenths of whom were employed*, have their insurance doctors and in many cases factory welfare supervisors which would combine to enforce a greater degree of fitness; moreover the women themselves attach supreme importance to the fitness of their husbands for their work.

(The account of this Peckham Health Centre investigation is contained in a report entitled *Biologists in Search of Material*. Faber and Faber, 2/-).

work can no longer be avoided. It would be unwise to demand a complete abandonment of this gallant disregard of her own aches and pains which is the result of her devotion to her task, and which is a part of the equipment of every person of sound mind and spirit; further, it would be absurd to expect that any woman should *always* feel and be perfectly well. But a middle course is surely possible which would educate her to a knowledge of such unhealthy conditions which are remediable within the pattern of her life, and in the cure of which she would become the efficient wife and mother which she so ardently strives to be. The knowledge and care would be protective as well as therapeutic, and would benefit her family as well as herself.

With these considerations clearly in mind, the diagnosis and incidence of disease recorded by these 1,250 women will be accepted with caution, but with the moral certainty that there is little or no *over-statement;* error, if it occurs, will consist in omission, rather than in commission. It is, for instance, certain that a far greater number of these women are anæmic than the 558 who specify this condition either by name or by some other indubitable symptoms; that many more of them suffer from carious teeth than the 165 whose bad teeth have either been detected by a doctor or have ached sufficiently to make disregard impossible. (Cf. notes attached to the analysis at the end of this chapter, of the seven most frequently mentioned ailments.) Even if the 392 women, who for lack of evidence to the contrary have been placed in the first, or good health group, had been examined by a doctor or verbally cross-questioned by anyone experienced in assessing the symptoms of physical unfitness, it is highly probable that very many of them would have been turned down into class 2 or even 3 or 4.

There are, however, some distinct differences between the environment of this first group and that of the women in the other health categories, which give ground for belief that some at least of the good health here recorded is not illusory. A much larger proportion of these women than that of the whole 1,250 is under 30 years of age; the average income is higher; more of them live in fairly good houses and have a fairly good diet; (*i.e. as housing and diet go in this investigation;* and in very few cases is a high standard of either reached;) and the average number of pregnancies is 3·8 instead of 4·5 for the whole 1,250.

Percentages compared between the ‚"good health" group and the whole 1,250.

	Percentage of whole 1,250 cases	Percentage of "good health group"
"Housekeeping"[1] money over 8/– per head per week	30	40.5
Good or fair housing	6.9	11.5
Apparently fair diet	33	66
Age under 30	26	35.2

It is clear therefore that a large number of the women in this group are living under conditions less remote from the basic necessities of good health than the other 858 women. Nevertheless there are some who, if the good health which they asseverate is a reality, must be of superhuman strength and vitality, for their lives appear as arduous and exhausting as those of any of the 1,250. 30 of these 392 women had nine or more pregnancies each. It is of interest to quote the records of a few of these.

Mrs. E. R. of Bethnal Green is 43 years old. She has had thirteen children, of whom eleven, ranging in age from 24 to 1½ years are living at home. She lives in a flat consisting of three rooms and a kitchen in a "short narrow street, poor district". Her husband is a dustman, and she has altogether £3 11s. 0d. "housekeeping money". She has to go two floors down into the yard for her *cold* water, and there is of course no hot water. She says she feels fit and well, and that her day's work is not too hard

[1] The phrase "housekeeping money," as used throughout this book is defined *as the total amount of money per week at the disposal of the housewife,* after the payment of rent. In general it covers food, light, coal, clothes for herself, and the children, hire-purchase payments for furniture, etc., clubs (for boots, etc.) and all insurance other than her husband's compulsory insurance.

for her, though she gets no leisure as the "children don't give me much time for leisure hours". Her only difficulties are that the washing has to go out as it is not convenient to do it at home, and she adds "Children are trying at times". She contributes 1d. a month to the Hospitals Savings Association.

Mrs. B. W. of Croydon is 38. She has had nine children all of whom are living at home; the eldest is 10, the youngest are twins of 6 months. She lives in a small cottage of four rooms and a scullery, which she says do not give them enough room; also she "would like a bathroom". Her only complaints as regards her health are constipation "on and off for twelve years", but as this only occurs when she is pregnant or breast-feeding, she does not attach much importance to it; and occasional indigestion due to the "rush over meals, as there is not much time after serving the family". She has been told to eat her meals dry, and now does so, finding it very beneficial. She has 24/– after paying rent (which is 18/–) on which to feed, clothe and warm the family. (She does not say whether *all* other household expenses come out of this, but as her husband is a contractor's carman, there is probably not much more than this coming in; but even if 24/– were for food alone . . .!) She is generally twelve hours a day on her feet, but at present as she is breast-feeding the twins, she gets "more rest". And in the evening she gets about two hours when she does her mending, darning, knitting or reading. She does not buy tinned or preserved foods, as she does "not find them economical with a family". She *never drinks tea*, but cocoa, made with water or tinned milk; or water; "am very fond of water". She has *apparently* a very good diet, which includes such delicacies as home-made fish paste, "as it is so much cheaper than bought". She is allowed from the Welfare Centre, while breast-feeding, two pints of milk and Ovaltine. The only difficulty she mentions is, "The house has a dirty old garden, it treads in house, and makes it so grubby; otherwise cannot complain, I am very fond of my home and take a pride in it so I am working most part of the day but am very happy".

And Mrs. MacN. of Glasgow, lives in one room and kitchen. She says it has *no* drawbacks. "I take everything as it comes, and the only difficulty is when baby is restless." Her husband is an unemployed carter, and she gets £2 unemployment money and 10/– from one boy (aged 16) who is working. Out of this £2 10s. 0d. she pays 9/– rent. She is 37 and has had 14 pregnancies, which include four children who have died and two miscarriages; there are therefore eight living children; five boys and two girls living at home; the eldest girl of 18 is married and "living in her own home". She is "never ill unless with children, and that passed off comfortably". She gets up at 6 and goes to bed at 10. Her leisure consists of "15 minutes round the block with baby till he goes to sleep; 15 minutes for messages at 2 p.m. Club gymnasium on Tuesday, 45 minutes, and sewing class Thursday one hour or so". Porridge and milk and vegetable soups are regular items of diet. The visitor who saw her says "This woman has absolutely no complaints about accommodation, health or lack of funds. She plans her time very methodically and manages to feed herself and her family sufficiently well to maintain health." The Scots are truly a wonderful people.

And as a last example of this remarkable set, Mrs. B. of Paddington; she occupies two "parlours" of a four-storied house, in a very thickly populated district. Her husband is a scavenger. She has to go downstairs for her water, and also to empty dirty water away. She is 48. She has had thirteen children and one miscarriage. Seven children live at home now, three are away and three have died. She has no leisure and a very poor diet. She gets up at 6 and goes to bed at 11. She says she is usually fit and well (which the visitor confirms), and to the question "Is your day's work too hard for you?" she answers, "Oh, No". The visitor adds that she "makes no trouble of any work"

As is seen in the case of Mrs. B. W. of Croydon, quoted above, trifling though recurrent ailments or more serious conditions which have been successfully treated have not disqualified a woman from being placed in this good health group. Only three women of this category say that they have suffered from anæmia. These were anæmic before marriage but affirm that they have been better since marriage; they do not say they have been *cured*. Twelve (seven in towns and five in the country) know that they have bad teeth; seven mention constipation; five, eyestrain; twelve complain of occasional headaches; seven suffer from indigestion occasionally, one from neuralgia and three from rheumatism. These are the only ailments mentioned at all.

The second group is of special interest as it contains a large majority of women who in spite of recording one or more chronic ailments, some of them serious, assert that they usually feel fit and well; they do not consider their condition morbid, but all the evidence given shows clearly that even by a moderate standard they are in poor health; a doctor would probably regard them as definitely ill. In this group there is a larger proportion of women with this attitude to their own health than in any other. For instance a woman at Cardiff aged 38 with eight children, who says she feels fit and well, admits to decayed teeth, bronchitis every winter, and prolapsed uterus ever since her second pregnancy. For neither of these last conditions has she had any treatment. Another in Battersea says she feels pretty well, but suffers from "internal trouble", (nature unspecified) which has lasted from the birth of her first child who is 10 years old; she is 31 and has had four children. She has "severe pains in the inside", but has not consulted anyone and takes no remedy. Such cases can be multiplied by the dozen.

The third and fourth group are both of women who are undoubtedly in very bad health, and the division between the two groups is necessarily very arbitrary. In the third group there is still found the stubborn affirmative answer to the question "Do you usually feel fit and well", but generally now with some such qualification as "Some-times", "Not too well", "On and off", "Fair". Mrs. A. of Birmingham is 30, has been married twelve years and has had ten children. She says "Fair" to the first question. She suffers from "swollen legs and veins", and "great weariness and headaches". She has been advised to go into hospital and to rest for the first, and to have her eyes tested for the second, and to have more fresh air. She cannot manage any of these remedies. She is intelligent, goes regularly to the Child Welfare Centre and so gets indirect advice about herself, but there the care of her health ends. Another woman in Cardiff says, "Not too well for last six years"; she has anæmia and rheumatism. She is 35 and has had nine children and one miscarriage. The cause of her anæmia she thinks is "having last few children rather too quickly". Four of the children have died, namely the fourth, fifth, sixth and seventh all born within the space of four years. Then came two more babies at an interval of one year exactly; these have survived. The Health Visitor writes "This is a poor type of mother, bad house manager and very sickly; children very unhealthy; husband has been out of work for some years. The mother does not seem to have enough energy to do anything properly".

There is little to choose as regards health between a woman in this position and those who have been put into the last group; in the latter there may be a larger number of ailments present, or they may be more serious; also here the women have for the most part reached the stage at which they can no longer ignore their condition; they *know* that they are ill, A fuller and apparently more correct diagnosis is generally given, because the condition is or has been so bad that professional advice, even if it is not taken, has at some time been asked.

INCIDENCE AND NATURE OF DISEASE.

The ailments of which there appears to be greatest incidence are:—

Anæmia ; this is specifically mentioned by the woman herself, or direct evidence of it is given by her and confirmed by the visitor, in 558 cases.

Headaches are mentioned in 291 cases. It is noticeable that where serious ailments are present, headaches are rarely mentioned, probably because they are overlooked when the woman knows she is in very poor health, or because they seem to her unimportant in comparison with her other conditions. It is however highly probably that they frequently occur in association with more serious disorders.

Constipation with or without hæmorrhoids is recorded in 273 cases. The same caution applies in accepting this as a complete figure. It is clearly looked upon as a very slight disorder, —and one to which in many cases the woman has become so accustomed that she does not notice its existence except when it results in severe pain.

Rheumatism is recorded by 258 women. This also is accepted as inevitable to a large extent, and is only treated in severe cases.

Gynæcological trouble of various kinds has occurred definitely in 191 cases; in a further 203 cases there appears evidence of it, but for various reasons no professional diagnosis has been made,—the woman herself is ignorant of the cause of her pain or discomfort.

Carious teeth and toothache are mentioned by 165 women only.

Varicose veins, ulcerated legs, white leg, phlebitis etc. are mentioned specifically by 101 women who say they have suffered acutely or been really crippled by such complaints. Many others speak of aching legs which would probably be medically diagnosed as one of these diseases.

These seven ailments have received special consideration in this chapter and have been fully analysed in relation to the woman's financial circumstances; treatment received, etc. etc. For each ailment only those cases have been taken where the definition can be relied upon.

Other ailments of which frequent mention is made are:— Backache, undiagnosed and unattributed to gynæcological trouble, kidneys or rheumatism; weak eyes or eye-strain; gastric trouble, indigestion, flatulence; neuritis and neuralgia; respiratory disorders, asthma, bronchitis, etc.; kidney trouble, cystitis, albuminuria, nephritis; cardiac trouble; bladder trouble; weariness and depression unattributed to any specific ailment; gallstones. There are also several recorded cases of deformity (one leg, one eye), and of deafness, thyroid trouble, mastoid, operations for appendicitis and other unspecified disorders, tonsils and adenoids, and last but not least tuberculosis of joints and bones as well as pulmonary.

TREATMENT.

Insurance. Only thirty-four out of the 1,250 women are doing paid work now, mostly part time. Of these, thirteen definitely say that they are insured under the National Health Insurance and use their panel doctor in illness; eight others say they use a panel doctor but say they are not insured; thirteen appear neither to be insured nor to use the panel doctor.[1]

Besides these there are sixty-five women who do not appear to do outside work, but who say they consult a panel doctor when they are ill. This is taken to mean that they employ their husbands' panel doctor, paying him for themselves.

About 55% contribute to the Hospital Savings Association or other hospital insurance schemes.

50% in the country and 7% in the towns contribute to the Nursing Association.

Other Medical Services used.

OTHER MEDICAL SERVICES USED

60% of the women consult a private doctor when ill.
8% consult Welfare Centres and/or Ante-natal Clinics.
6% consult the Public Assistance or Parish Doctor;
3% consult the Health Visitor and/or District Nurse.

[1] It seems clear that many women who do part-time work are not insured, or say they are not insured because their employers only pay contributions. (A woman mainly dependent on someone else may herself be exempt from N.H.I. contributions.)

3% consult the out-patient departments of hospitals.
        (These appear also to include those who attend Ante-
        natal Clinics held at a Hospital).
2% consult a chemist.

Many of these services overlap. For instance, a woman
who has a private doctor for her serious ailments will
also go to the Ante-natal Clinic when she is pregnant. It will
be seen that by no means all the women in the sample are
included in these figures.

For some ailments and in some places there is great
difficulty in getting treatment. Eye and dental treatments
in country places bristle with obstacles. Neither a dentist
nor an oculist comes to a patient's house, and in some
country places transport difficulties are insuperable. Forty-
seven women out of 165 who have bad teeth have had no
advice or treatment at all; of these, thirty-five live in the
country, and twenty-five give as a reason for not taking
advice that they cannot get to the dentist. Bad teeth and
bad sight are not considered illnesses in themselves either
by the public Health Authority or by the woman herself,
and consequently she cannot get free ambulance transport.

READINESS TO TAKE ADVICE.

As will be more fully discussed in the next chapter
women show a general disinclination to fuss about themselves, which is the result partly of their exhausting work,
partly of their preoccupation with the welfare of their
families and partly of ignorance, or a curious failure to apply
to themselves what they do know about health in general.
Advice therefore is not sought as often as it should be, or if
sought is not taken. In the seven ailments specially analysed,
advice and treatment have been divided into four categories.
    There are the women who:—

1. Ask advice and follow it.
2. Ask advice and do not follow it.
3. Take only "home" or chemist's remedies.
4. Take no advice or remedy.

The most important controlling factor in this is poverty, especially in those illnesses which the woman thinks she can fairly safely overlook, such as headaches, constipation, anæmia and bad teeth. Here is a typical example of this attitude, governed by lack of funds. A woman in Preston aged 30 has had three children, the eldest of whom died in infancy. Her husband is unemployed. She has 27/3 housekeeping money, and is in a very bad house, which has no sink. She suffers from constipation, headaches, faintness and "low condition". "I go to bed early with the children and get up late to save coal and food." She says, "I went to see Clinic Doctor. She advised me to go to own Doctor and get a tonic, said I was under-nourished and run down, owe Doctor 2 accounts so shall not go." Another example comes from Mrs. F. of Sheffield. She is 47 and has had seven children, of whom two have died. Her husband is a railway drayman. She gets £2 17s. 0d. housekeeping (including £1 from one son of 23 who lives at home "but eats a lot".) She has rheumatism, (since she had an operation for gall-stones two years ago,) toothache, headache and back-ache. For none of these does she consult anyone. She owes her private doctor for the last five years' attendance, including the last confinement, £14, which she pays off in 1/– weekly instalments collected by a collector. The Health Visitor says, "I think there is no doubt a good deal of this woman's ailments are due to her very bad teeth; she is terrified at the idea of a dentist."

Rheumatism, gynæcological troubles and bad legs being much more crippling to work, show a larger percentage of advice sought and treatment taken. Gynæcological trouble has other features in respect of treatment. The woman probably does not recognise the symptoms herself. ("Backache since birth of baby". "Internal trouble through confinements", are frequent complaints for which no advice and treatment have been sought,) and in the absence of a thorough post-natal examination, the trouble is not discovered till the birth of the next child, often not then if she has not been attended by a doctor. When it *is* discovered, much greater pressure is brought to bear on her by the doctor or nurse to have the matter attended to. An example of this is given by a Manchester woman of 35 who has three children. She has had very bad backache since her first confinement, and at her second confinement the doctor diagnosed a prolapse and advised an operation. She could not face this then, but the condition has got worse since the birth of the third child, and she is now "waiting for the bed in the hospital". Another similar case of a Norfolk woman of 34 with three children, who has had prolapse since her first child. She is very poor and lives in an extremely bad house. She had no treatment till after the third child, and then the uterus was stitched. She was six weeks in hospital and two weeks at a convalescent home.

The comparative percentages for professional treatment in the seven specially analysed ailments are:—

Headaches	30%	are professionally treated.	
Constipation.	36%	,,	,,	,,
Anæmia.	38%	,,	,,	,,
Bad teeth.	43%	,,	,,	,,
Rheumatism.	56%	,,	,,	,,
Gynæcological trouble	59%	,,	,,	,,
Bad Legs	60%	,,	,,	,,

The best of these figures shows a deplorably low percentage of treatment and it is not entirely explained by poverty, or a courageous neglect. There is also a good deal of prejudice and/or fear due to ignorance. This is apparent particularly in cases where hospital treatment, an operation or otherwise, is needed, and also with bad teeth. Out of 165 women who know they have bad teeth, 94 have either not sought advice or not taken the advice given; of these 94, 26 admit to being afraid of going to the dentist, and in several other cases the nurse or health visitor speaks of having tried in vain to persuade the woman to have her teeth seen to.

The Essex woman quoted on p. 76 of the next chapter has a "horror of hospitals". Another country woman aged 41, very poor, with four children, and a very bad house, has a "torn lower bowel and dropped womb" and she says of both "These could be righted in hospital, but don't like the idea." The bowel trouble dates from her first confinement, the prolapse from her second. There is also a great deal of ignorant prejudice. A woman with fibroid on the uterus has been advised to have hysterectomy performed, but her husband is unwilling. She is 38 and has eight children already. A woman of 36 with ten children refuses to go to hospital for "uterine trouble" . . . "because of children". The Health Visitor says she has argued with her after each confinement, but it is useless, "I think it is prejudice". Another aged 36 has seven children, and has an ovarian cyst, and an operation has been advised, but she doesn't "like hospitals". Another with severe vaginal discharge, which has lasted some years, has had seven children. She says she "would consult a Doctor for a definite illness, which would have to be paid for out of housekeeping money". A woman from an outlying district of London describes how she heard a lecture about a Woman's Clinic in the centre and determined to go there in preference to the out-patient department of her hospital which she had been attending for some weeks. She writes:—"I went to the centre (the Woman's Clinic) because I did not like to go to hospital again. I went after my operation, but they have no proper women's out-patient department and the man doctor used to come out to me in the waiting-room and asked me how I was feeling. I could not tell him why I had come to see him as I had two youths sitting beside me, so I said I was quite well and went away. I cannot go to the doctor who told me to go to the hospital; I only went to him first because I didn't know where else to go. He is a young bachelor and will not examine me unless I take someone with me and as I have no friends on the new estate this is too difficult; besides I can't talk to a young man about such intimate affairs. I think a woman must have a woman doctor for these things, and we would not have so much trouble if we did." This is not prejudice, but a clear indication of where the medical service for women needs development.

THE EFFICACY OF TREATMENT.

An even sadder story of the efforts to cure ill-health is given by the records of the inefficacy of treatment. Over and over again the woman is unable to continue a treatment begun, either because it involves too much expense, or a weekly visit to a hospital and hours of waiting for which she cannot spare the time. Almoners and Health Visitors who have added notes show disappointment in the woman's improvement after treatment, but the one method of treatment which seems to have a magical effect is three or four weeks convalescence at the sea.

THE DOCTOR'S ADVICE.

The professional advice that the women receive appears to vary greatly in value. It is noticeable that many who have consulted their own doctor for such an ailment as bad backache or anæmia have been told to change their diet, to eat more nourishing food, to rest more, to sleep more and to get more fresh air. The changes are rung on these remedies over and over again.

A woman in Leeds who has had nine children of whom the seventh and eighth have died, has 44/- a week housekeeping money, and a poor house; she suffers from anæmia, neurasthenia and loss of appetite. She has a private doctor who "advises rest, nourishment and not to worry". A widow in Maidenhead with four young children has heart trouble; she is obviously a very delicate woman; she has been told that she "must take things easy". Another in London with six children says "My Doctor before each child advised always rest and usually bed which is practically impossible."

There appears to be only one remedy for bad teeth, and that is extraction. This may be because extractions are free for those who contribute to the Hospital Savings Association or other hospital insurance schemes. A great many women say that they either won't have their teeth out because they can't afford new ones, or have had them out in spite of the inability to pay for new set. Mrs. L. A. of Leeds, aged 34 suffers from sick headaches and biliousness since she had all her teeth drawn six years ago, and she thinks the inability to masticate her food properly accounts for these ailments; she writes, "My husband was in good and regular work when I had my teeth out at the general Infirmary and I paid 10/– towards false ones and then my husband had to give up his work owing to operation and he has not worked since, and I have not paid any further on them, and I haven't bothered since knowing I could not afford to pay for them."

Contraceptive advice seems practically non-existent. A few women in London, Rotherham and Devonshire speak of having been to the Birth Control Clinics, but there are dozens of women in obvious need of such advice either for procuring proper intervals between births, or to have no more children, who, although they have been told by their doctor that this is necessary, are not instructed by him in scientific methods and do not go to a Birth Control Clinic, even if there is one within reach. This seems to indicate a deplorable ignorance or prejudice on the part of the professional medical attendant. It is noticeable that in Birmingham for instance many of these cases occur. Three examples may be given. Mrs. H. is 35 and has had eight children (one of whom died). She has bad varicose veins which she puts down to repeated pregnancies, and anæmia which has become acute in the last four years, due "mostly to poverty and malnutrition". For this she gets "an occasional iron tonic from family Doctor". He has also advised her to "eat more fruit and vegetables and to have less children". This advice at the best seems a little belated ! Mrs. W. R. lives in a very poor house. She is 30 and has had ten children (one set of twins) of whom two have died. Her husband has been unemployed for four years. She was in hospital five weeks for phlebitis, and she has swollen legs and veins and very bad headaches "always". The Midwife, Doctor and Health Visitor advised hospital for her legs which advice she took, but they are still bad; they also advised rest, but she has ten in her household and 30/6 housekeeping money. Mrs. A. is 45; she has had twelve children and one miscarriage. Her youngest child is a month old. Nine children live at home, seven of them are under 14 years, and the home is a back-to-back house consisting of three rooms. She consults a private doctor for herself and her children, and contributes to the Nursing Association; so that she is not without professional advice. Her housekeeping money is 30/-, out of which she pays the rent of 8/6. She has an appalling diet, potatoes, an occasional sausage and greens once a week being the only additions to "b & b & t" (bread and butter and tea). Birmingham has several Birth Control Clinics.

There is a woman in Sheffield who has had five Cæsarian sections; all the children but one have lived. She, too, lives in a back-to-back house. She has had rheumatic fever and says that the five Cæsarians have drained all her vitality.

There appears also to be lack of skill or knowledge in dealing with certain types of ailments. For instance the Rotherham woman (quoted again on p. 92 of the next chapter) writes that her doctor says "all women get backache round about 40, so why worry." A woman of 43 who has had ten children and three miscarriages (four children have died), has had bad hæmorrhage for nine years; this has resulted in a weak heart. Her doctor puts it down to a "certain age", and tells her to rest in bed ! Her husband is on transitional benefit. Twenty-seven women in indifferent or poor health, who are between 40 and 45 attribute some of their ailments to change of life or "a certain age". Another woman consulted her doctor about dysmenorrhœa; he was "rather off-hand about it and told me that as I was small made and that was the reason". Another on the same subject says, "My experience is that doctors are not sympathetic about this. All my doctor says is that I grew too quickly and shall grow out of it. I have not done so yet and am nearly 25."

HEALTH TEACHING.

404 or about 32·3% of all the women say that they have had no health teaching whatever. 156 of these are in the first group (good health). Of the remaining 846, 64 say they had some teaching at home, 62 at school. Apparently this teaching was of the simplest kind such as "early to bed and early to rise", or "to keep yourself clean" or "deep breathing".

A country woman in Northumberland says that she had no health teaching at School or elsewhere, but adds "A good manners chart hung on the wall (at school); possibly it had some instructions on it." These and the remainder have learnt anything they know from Welfare Centres and Ante-natal Clinics (591 women cite these), the Health Visitor and/or District Nurse (245 cases); Daily Press; magazines, wireless, lectures at Clubs, Church Socials, etc. (217 cases), and their own doctor (67 cases). Eleven women have been nurses or midwives and therefore have had some special training.

A curious phenomenon appears when comparing the figures of advice sought, with those of health teaching received. Although over 70% of the women say they *consult* a doctor in illness (i.e. private, panel or parish doctor; see p. 38), only about 5% speak of having had any *health teaching* from a doctor, and conversely although only 8% *consult* Ante-natal or other Welfare Centres, 47% speak of having *learnt about health* at such Clinics; and though only 3% *consult* the District Nurse, and Health Visitor, 20% have received *teaching* from such officers.

The explanation of this is implicit in all the information the women give. In general the mother is a great deal more careful and anxious to learn about the health of the children than about her own. The large majority of attendances "at the Clinic" for instance, are at Infant Welfare Centres to which she takes her babies. She does not therefore mention these in her answer to the question "whom do you consult when *you* feel ill". She is very often not conscious of having consulted them about herself, because the object of her visit is her children. Advice given to her for herself is incidental and often unsought. And even when no such advice is given, she picks up a good deal of knowledge about health in general, which she may or may not apply to herself. There are certain simple but sound rules of good health, not beyond the poorest woman's capacity to obey, which can be directly traced to the Clinics, such as drinking a good deal of water, the value of open windows, etc., etc.

The same applies to the country districts where to a very large extent the District Nurse or Health Visitor (the two functions are often combined in one person) takes the place of the Welfare Centre. She is in constant and regular attendance at the cottage home for the purpose of weighing infants, and attending to the health of the pre-school children. She will also know when a mother is pregnant and be able to advise on care and diet and, if necessary, to give the order for free milk. It is reasonable therefore that the mother should learn a great deal about health in general without consciously consulting the Nurse about herself. The value to the health of the mother of these opportunities for observation of her by experienced Nurses, Welfare Centre doctors or Health Visitors cannot be over estimated. The indirect approach to the subject of herself puts her at her ease, and she is not conscience-stricken about "having made a fuss". A private or panel doctor stands in a very different relationship to her. Although she may consult him whenever she feels there is real need either for herself or her children, he is only called in in dire necessity and to attend a particular ailment. The professional medical man (or woman) is not communicative to his patient even about the illness he is treating, far less about matters of health unrelated either to the illness in question or to the patient he happens to be attending. He does not sit down as the Health Visitor or nurse does, and watch the baby being nursed or bathed and talk to the mother at the same time. If he is attending another member of the family, he does not in all probability *observe* the mother, for in the first place the patient is by hypothesis really ill (and the mother therefore worried and pre-occupied), and secondly it is considered unprofessional to offer unsought advice. The function of the doctor in these circumstances is merely therapeutic; that of the Welfare Centre prophylactic.

There is in addition another reason that the private doctor is not or cannot be as helpful in health teaching as these other agencies. He is in most cases a man. The mother is not as much at her ease with a man as with a woman. She is first of all more afraid of being told that she is making a fuss about nothing, then she is too shy to talk to a man about certain ailments which may involve reference to parts of her body about which she has been taught she must never speak; and she feels instinctively that he cannot understand her difficulties as a woman can. Of course there are exceptions. The family doctor is sometimes a real friend and confidant. But it is obvious that on the whole the women feel much less embarrassment and fear in talking to a woman, be she the visiting Health Officer, Midwife or District Nurse, or the lay workers, nurse or doctor (who is generally a woman) at the Welfare Centre (see quotation above, p. 42).

The letter, appended to this chapter, from a District Nurse who is also the Midwife and Health Visitor for six villages in an agricultural district confirms these observations.

Health Before and After Marriage.

It is likely that more ill-health was present before marriage than is here recorded, and to a certain extent this can be confirmed by the 60 forms from unmarried women which were received (but not analysed; see p. 25). Many of them say that they do not knock off work when they feel ill. One of them writes "There are many girls who work (especially piece-workers) when obviously a few days off would put them right. Then again plenty of people value money more than health. Speed is the great thing in industry. . . . It plays havoc with most people's lives. . . . In the winter we often work over (overtime) one hour a day, and it makes a tremendous difference to many girls, one feels like going to bed of an evening instead of doing something interesting."

This desire not to lose money together with the lack of teaching on health and a great reluctance to speak about health would combine to make a girl go on working and to think she was normally well, when in reality she was far from fit. Certainly more anæmia was present before marriage than has been recognised by the 1,250 women, and conditions such as dysmenorrhœa were and still are so much taken for granted that they were not considered ailments by the working girl.

But making every allowance for the understatement of pre-marital ill-health, it is clear that by far the greater part of the sickness described by the women of this investigation has occurred after the birth of the first child. The answer "Not since I married" is a common one to the question "Do you usually feel fit and well?" (see Mrs. L. C. of Cardiff and Mrs. L. of Bromley on page 79 of next chapter), and to the question of the duration of a complaint, "Since the first or second pregnancy". There is unquestionably greater incidence of ill-health amongst the women with a large number of pregnancies, and consequently with the greatest weight of physical and financial responsibility. This is a proof that it is the cumulative effect of years of ever-increasing toil which even if it results in no definite disease (or in none that they can specify) crushes the vitality of so many working mothers, and reduces them too often by the age of 40 or 50 to a grievous and irremediable state of health.

Here is a revealing description by a woman who has no very serious illness, and does not grumble much about health, but none the less is being worn down by an accumulation of small ailments, a large family and "worry". She lives at Thornton Heath in a self-contained flat, three rooms and a scullery. She is only 35, has been married fourteen years and has had eight children and one miscarriage; one child has died. So there are now nine people in the family and she has £2 2s. 6d. for housekeeping after the payment of rent (7/6). She says she does "not always feel fit and well". She has piles and constipation which have lasted nine years, due she thinks to childbirth. "Well, I have tried Nutgall ointment and also have taken liquid parifin which I found to ease me—I have had advice from our Health Visitor, her advice being Liquid Parifin and Bathe with cold water. Also taken X lax and Beacham Pills. Rheumatism 2 years. I think the cause of it is because the ilconvient of dry washing in the living room and also having a gas cooker in it. I have put a large Portion of scelery in stews and soup. Had advice from one of our welfare ladies and was given some Black Paist to apply to Painful Parts which gave much relief. Bad hearing for 4 years, the living room is the cause which causes a terrible lot of steam and dampness. I have used Proxide and had so many drops twice a day." She gets up at 6.45 and goes to bed at 11. She is on her feet fourteen to sixteen hours a day. She says of her leisure that she has between "2 and 3 hours and I can alway find Plenty a Darning and Patching if not that I am refooting sock and Knitting them and Jumpers for the Kiddies and half a day I spend at Welfare that being the longest Rest I have." She appears to be sensible about diet and drinks a lot of water, but she eats only one egg a week, and boiled fish once a week. The "special difficulties" are "sleeping accommodation and want of a larger and lighter kitchen without a gas cooker in for you get all the steam and heat which takes you of your food also not surfactant money to run your House Hold proply also Having to Dry colthes in living when wether is wet." And she writes on the back of the form, "From the time I was married up until about 4 years ago I shared fairly good health except when in Pregnancy, when I think your nerves get Bad owing the tiersome tricks of the children and just little worry's my Health began to get bad about 4 years ago when I was sent away for a change to Eastbourne that rest and Plenty a good food and no worry of the other children I began to feel myself again, than after I had been home a while I began to get Bad Headache and this I think is reaaly being shut up in such a small flat with such a large family and when all the Doors are shut it is so dark and depressing that is what makes your nerves bad and too many sleeping in one room and not being able to have the windows open surfacant to let the bad air out and the fresh in because of the draught. I think my health would enprov if I had a larger place and more fentilation."

In contrast to this there are a very few women who say they have felt much stronger since marriage. The wife of a South Wales miner was "always ailing before marriage", but says now she has very good health. She has five children well spaced, and is comparatively well off. Mrs. H. of Birmingham aged 36 has two children. She had bad anæmia and bad dysmenorrhœa when she was 16 and onwards, but went to a women's hospital for treatment and is much better since the birth of her first child. A woman in Rotherham who was a clerk before marriage and suffered a good deal, mostly, she thinks through the sedentary occupation, says:—"Since marriage I have felt better as regards my health and show it outwardly. I am sure the reason is I am in and out of doors more not closed in an office for hours". She has only one child and a fairly good income.

Excessive Child Bearing.

There is curiously little evidence here of that fall of the birth-rate about which the nation is becoming so rightly alarmed. It is merely fortuitous however that these 1,250 women have been collected from a section whose *admitted* average pregnancies are nearly five. This is a very high figure compared to that for the whole population, and after allowing for the admitted miscarriages and still-births the average number of children born alive is over four per family. This would not be too high a figure if the parents were in a financial position to provide the standard of housing, clothing, diet and general well-being which are the birth-right of every child, and if the mother were not forced, through lack of knowledge, funds and facilities to neglect her own welfare, becoming as a rule with the arrival of each child a slightly less efficient agent in the maintenance of the family well-being.

221 women admit to eight pregnancies or more each, and there is ample evidence that pregnancies are not over-stated. There are the living children who can be counted (sometimes it has been noticed, with difficulty) and the dead ones are generally remembered, whereas a mis-carriage or a still-birth, particularly in a large family, may easily be overlooked.

In spite of this very high birthrate, only 29 women out of the 1,250 seem to be aware that too many or too frequent pregnancies may be the cause of, or contribute to, their unfitness, lassitude, or definite illnesses. An increase in the family brings with it so many additional difficulties in daily life, that the mother thinks that the waning of her strength is due rather to the extra work than to the wear and tear of child-birth, which is anyhow a "natural and normal" process. Here are some of the few exceptions to this attitude. Mrs. A. T. of Heston is 25 and has had five children in five years of marriage. She ¡was anæmic before marriage, and she is very bad indeed now "through having five children so quickly and not getting enough rest after being confined".

Mrs. Y. of S. Wales has five children of whom the eldest is 4½. As her only difficulty she says, "I have had children too quickly after each other and with young children they take up all my time. Am unable to breast feed". The Health Visitor says "Mrs. Y. looks in very poor condition, she says she always feels tired and disinclined to do anything. I think she was probably anæmic before marriage and five pregnancies in five years have drained her vitality."

The wife of an unemployed steel-bender in Newcastle with seven children has headaches and strained heart and has just recovered from a bad attack of pleurisy. She says "too frequent child-bearing " is the main cause. She was studying to be a teacher before marriage and was "perfectly healthy".

And Mrs. A. of Battersea is 48 and has had twenty children and one stillbirth in 30 years. She gets up at 6.30 and goes to bed at midnight. The Health Visitor says "One of the children (in addition to the still-birth) died when young and one daughter at the age of 20 on the birth of *her* second child. This daughter was the mother of a boy now aged 11 and a girl aged 9, included in the lot of children living at home. Four children are married and living away so that the household now consists of the mother and father and sixteen children of whom two are grandchildren ! The mother's own youngest child is 4. (i.e. many years younger than her grandchildren !) One of the difficulties mentioned by the mother is "seating at mealtimes"! There is "no bathroom, and the kitchen is too small". She suffers from debility which came on after the last pregnancy" (four years ago), and is due she says to "multiple pregnancies".

And Mrs. W. of E. London is 43, has had twenty-two pregnancies, thirteen children and nine miscarriages; she has suffered from anæmia, kidney trouble and heart trouble for years. She has had Hospital advice, but apparently no Birth Control. Her youngest child is 4. She thinks she has had "rather too many children".

But the wife of an Essex market gardener is 34 years old and has eleven children all under 15. She says she is perfectly well and has no complaints except that there is "no water indoors".

Conclusion

Very great appreciation of the public medical services is expressed by those women who use them, particularly of the women officers, lay or medical. But it is clear that the services are not used nearly as much as they might be, and that there are serious gaps in them which the private doctor is inadequate to bridge. To begin with there is no systematic training in the rules of good health while the girl is young, nor,—which is a more serious omission,— when she is about to become a mother. The Ante-natal Clinic too often fails to get hold of the mother in her first pregnancy, and she embarks on this adventure without even the rudiments of scientific knowledge. Even if the Health Visitor, Doctor or Nurse is able to persuade her to make full use of the Infant Welfare Centre for her baby, and of the Ante-natal clinic in her next pregnancy, she has lost the golden opportunity of her life for equipping herself for the efficient discharge of the responsibilities and duties which will absorb her for the next twenty years or more. When she marries she generally gives up her paid work. She has not yet the care of the children, and she might in that year acquire knowledge which would be invaluable to her in preserving her own health as well as in looking after her family.

Even the Ante-natal Clinic, excellent though its help can be, is deficient in giving the mother the practical experience she might be acquiring. Lectures and demonstrations on the care of the baby as well as on the care of herself would form a most useful addition to the educative functions of such a clinic. Further, if the importance of this had been impressed upon her as a girl or when she was about to be married, a much larger proportion of young women would attend such clinics in their first pregnancy.

It is of the utmost importance that there should be clinics to cover all the periods of the working mother's life, both before and after marriage. It should not be necessary in order to receive such help as they can give, for her to have started on her career of motherhood or to have a child still young enough to go to an Infant Welfare Centre. The clinics should be for her as well as for the children, and should be ready to give her advice, treatment and active practical help in any of the problems which affect her health and happiness.

Clinics appear to fill a need for which no other medical agency is as good. As sorting stations for the Hospitals they would be invaluable, and equally for providing through a specialised staff that expert knowledge on particular aspects of the woman's problem which the private doctor so often lacks. The hospitals are too awe-inspiring, too impersonal and remote, and too important to discharge the humble function of that sort of friendly inquisition which usually takes place at the clinic, or during the visit of the District Nurse (the travelling Clinic of the country.) A Doctor has to be paid, a visit to a hospital may involve a journey which is costly in time and money, and *as only a very few of these women have anything at all left over for such luxuries as medical advice, it must be available to them free or for the cost of a few pence.* And again at the Clinic the mother finds the atmosphere is easier and pleasanter; very often the consultant is a woman like herself, and will meet her halfway in the difficult recital of her grievances. The confidence that the mother has in the right kind of medical adviser is capable of

infinite development and encouragement, and there should
be no difficulty in her day's work, her domestic problems
or her own and her family's welfare for which she should
not be able to find immediately and at close range sympathetic, expert, and, if necessary, gratuitous counsel. This
is the least that can be offered to alleviate the burdens of
a life which even in the happiest possible circumstances
is one of gruelling hard work.

Medical Birth Control advice should be available for
every working woman in order that she should be given
at least the chance to protect herself, *and her family*, from
the terrible state of attrition that is bound to be the result
of too quick successive pregnancies or pregnancies more
numerous than the mother has strength to bear, or the
father to provide for. There is no greater personal tragedy
and no greater national danger than that the arrival of
each new baby should be (however "natural and inevitable") an intolerable burden for the parents. It has been
said that the value of the "working" man's labour is not
high enough to provide for a family of more than one or
perhaps two children. If that is so (and it might be argued
that under a different economic system it would not be
so,) then first and foremost the State must provide not
only greater protection for maternal health, but an adequate
economic subsidy for the growing family. Even so the
parents should be in a position to *decide* how many children
they can have. That such knowledge should not be available
to women in the circumstances of the 1,250 under review
is a serious indictment of the care given by the State to
the mothers and children of the present generation. The
mother's unwillingness to complain is no excuse. Her
loyalty to and love for her children are the reason for this,
but this only makes the tragedy of the position greater for
her. However much she presses herself on, she *cannot*
keep her pace when at each lap owing to decreased resist-
ance she needs more time to recover. The exhaustion,
both of funds and of strength, does not proceed by equal

stages with the arrival of each child, but by a terrible geometrical progression. The whole family is thrust deeper into poverty, the standard of well-being is forced down for all of them, and in addition to the original demand made upon the mother's resources in the bearing of the child, she is the member of the family who will be most heavily taxed, in labour, in health and in the basic necessities of life. The unborn child is almost as exacting as the living one, and although it is not for one moment alleged that an enormous number of the children also are not ill-fed, ill-housed and ill-provided for, it is undeniable that a great part of what they do receive of mental and physical well-being is at the sacrifice of their mothers. "The calf destroys the flanks of its mother."

FULLER ANALYSIS OF THE SEVEN MOST FREQUENTLY MENTIONED AILMENTS.

N.B.—As has been said before, the figures of incidence of all these ailments are likely to be too low. But the analysis is none the less useful in demonstrating how each of the ailments is treated by the women themselves and professionally; also the relation they bear to the general conditions of the woman's life.

1. ANAEMIA. 558 cases

Average pregnancies . . 5.6

80 out of the 558 were admittedly anæmic before marriage.
202 out of the 558 live in very bad houses.
310 out of the 558 appear to have a totally inadequate diet.

Income and Treatment

193 with 4/- and under per head per week "housekeeping" money	of these	45 have had advice and followed it
		20 have had advice and not followed it
		23 use home remedies
		105 take no advice or remedy

229 with 4/1—6/- per head per week "housekeeping" money	of these	100 have had advice and followed it
		26 have had advice and not followed it
		18 use home remedies
		85 take no advice or remedy

Income and Treatment

95
with 6/1—8/-
per head per week
"housekeeping"money
⎱ of these ⎰
44 have had advice and followed it
8 have had advice and not followed it
13 use home remedies
30 take no advice or remedy

27
with 8/1—10/-
per head per week
"housekeeping"money
⎱ of hese ⎰
18 have had advice and followed it
1 has had advice and not followed it
3 use home remedies
5 take no advice or remedy

14
with over 10/-
per head per week
"housekeeping"money
⎱ of these ⎰
10 have had advice and followed it
1 has had advice and not followed it
None use home remedies
3 take no advice or remedy

2. HEADACHES. 291 cases

(N.B. These do not include the women who say they have occasional or slight headaches).

Income and Treatment

59
with 4/- and under
per head per week
"housekeeping"money
⎱ of these ⎰
6 have had advice and followed it
5 have had advice and not followed it
6 use home remedies
22 take no advice or remedy

110
with 4/1—6/-
per head per week
"housekeeping"money
⎱ of these ⎰
49 have had advice and followed it
8 have had advice and not followed it
46 use home remedies
47 take no advice or remedy

68
with 6/1—8/-
per week per head
"housekeeping"money
⎱ of these ⎰
21 have had advice and followed it
4 have had advice and not followed it
2 use home remedies
41 take no advice or remedy

39
with 8/1—10/-
per head her week
"housekeeping"money
⎱ of these ⎰
9 have had advice and followed it
4 have had advice and not followed it
6 use home remedies
20 take no advice or remedy

16
with over 10/-
per head per week
"housekeeping"money
⎱ of these ⎰
8 have had advice and followed it
None have had advice and not followed it
2 use home remedies
6 take no advice or remedy

Home remedies consist almost entirely of "Aspros".

38 cases appear to be caused by eye-strain, and of these eleven say they have been advised to have glasses but cannot afford them. One seems satisfied with a pair

of Woolworth glasses ! One says the headaches are caused by her parents living in the house and "should be got rid off".

One woman says her eyes are hurt by the light when she goes out of her "dark smelly kitchen".

51 say they have always had bad headaches.

Apart from these a large proportion of headaches start fairly soon after marriage, and the same proportion of headaches persist through all the different age groups. The most frequent association of headaches with other ailments is with constipation, anæmia and eye-strain.   If headaches occur in association with the complaints that the woman herself thinks serious, they are very little mentioned.

3. CONSTIPATION AND/OR HÆMORRHOIDS.   273 cases

Average pregnancies.   5.
85 say they were constipated before marriage.
87 live in very bad houses.
147 appear to have very bad diet.

The cause most frequently given is pregnancy. One woman speaks of "Indiscriminate dosings in childhood" as the cause. Some say they have not time to establish a regular habit, or that they cannot find the closet vacant when they have time to go. A few give the cause as lack of sufficient or of the right kind of food.

Income and treatment

38 with 4/- and under per head per week "housekeeping" money	} of these {	8 have had advice and followed it 1 has had advice and not followed it 25 use home remedies 4 take no advice or remedy
96 with 4/1—6/- per head per week "housekeeping" money	} of these {	34 have had advice and followed it None have had advice and not followed it 46 use home remedies 16 take no advice or remedy
70 with 6/1—8/- per head per week "housekeeping" money	} of these {	26 have had advice and followed it 1 has had advice and not followed it 32 use home remedies 11 take no advice or remedy
28 with 8/1—10/- per head per week "housekeeping" money	} of these {	9 have had advice and followed it 1 has had advice and not followed it 11 use home remedies 7 take no advice or remedy

41
with over 10/-
per head per week
"housekeeping"money

of these

22 have had advice and followed it
None have had advice and not
          followed it
17 use home remedies
2 take no advice or remedy

There is little *apparent* connection between bad sanitation and constipation. This is probably because constipation is not mentioned when there are other serious disorders, which are more frequent in bad housing conditions, i.e. where there is bad sanitation. Diet, however, appears to be a far more frequent cause.

4. CARIOUS TEETH AND TOOTHACHE. 165 cases

Average pregnancies. 5.
25 had bad teeth before marriage.
57 in bad houses.

Treatment consists almost entirely of extraction, and sometimes the woman cannot afford a new set.

Income and Treatment

30
with 4/- and under
per head per week
"housekeeping"money

of these

11 have had advice and followed it
11 have had advice and not followed it
3 use home remedies
5 take no advice or remedy

86
with 4/1—6/-
per head per week
"housekeeping"money

of these

37 have had advice and followed it
26 have had advice and not followed it
3 use home remedies
20 take no advice or remedy

31
with 6/1—8/-
per head per week
"housekeeping"money

of these

15 have had advice and followed it
5 have had advice and not followed it
None use home remedies
11 take no advice or remedy

11
with 8/1—10/-
per head per week
"housekeeping"money

of these

3 have had advice and followed it
3 have had advice and not followed it
None use home remedies
5 take no advice or remedy

7
with over 10/-
per head per week
"housekeeping"money

of these

5 have had advice and followed it
2 have had advice and not followed it
None use home remedies
None take no advice or remedy

5. RHEUMATISM. 258 cases

39 of these say they have had rheumatic fever

Average pregnancies. 5·9.
92 in bad houses (the average pregnancies for these is 6·5).
159 of these women had no rheumatism before the age of 35.
A great many speak of rheumatism as "hereditary".

Income and Treatment

35 with 4/– and under per head per week "housekeeping"money	of these	15 have had advice and followed it
		7 have had advice and not followed it
		4 use home remedies
		9 take no advice or remedy

90 with 4/1—6/– per head per week "housekeeping"money	of these	52 have had advice and followed it
		4 have had advice and not followed it
		7 use home remedies
		27 take no advice or remedy

61 with 6/1—8/– per head per week "housekeeping"money	of these	38 have had advice and followed it
		6 have had advice and not followed it
		7 use home remedies
		10 take no advice or remedy

29 with 8/1—10/– per head per week "housekeeping"money	of these	21 have had advice and followed it
		None have had advice and not followed it
		2 use home remedies
		6 take no advice or remedy

43 with 10/– and over per head per week "housekeeping"money	of these	22 have had advice and followed it
		1 has had advice and not followed it
		10 use home remedies
		10 take no advice or remedy

Home remedies mentioned are "hot flannels",—"keeping parts warm",—"rubbing with oil", and various patent medicines.

6. GYNÆCOLOGICAL AILMENTS. 191 cases

Average pregnancies. 5·2.
29 Women under the age of 30.
108 women between 30 and 39.

It is difficult to analyse with any accuracy the gynæcological ailments. For instance a woman speaks of albuminuria, and puts the cause down to childbirth but does not say whether the condition has persisted; or mentions "uterine trouble", "internal trouble", etc., and says pregnancy is the cause, but gives no further particulars: "Severe hæmorrhage" is often mentioned but no other details.

Complete accuracy is therefore not claimed for the following analysis, as a medical report would possibly

have placed the ailments in different categories. Some
women have more than one of the following conditions.

Dysmenorrhœa   8 cases.   (2 before marriage).
Menorrhagia   12 cases.   (3 before marriage).
Backache   56 cases.   10 associated with kidney trouble
                                      during or after pregnancy.
                            29 "severe since child birth."
                            14 attributed to prolapse.
                             3 unspecified, but examinatic
                            advised.

Uterine prolapse   30 cases
Puerperal fever   4 cases
"Womb trouble"   15 cases
    unspecified
Severe post-partum hæmorrhage   10 cases
Breast abscess, mastitis, etc.   9 cases
Leucorrhœa   11 cases.
Kidney Diseases, associated with pregnancy   29 cases.
(besides those under backache)
Ulcerated uterus   15 cases
Post-natal Operations   35 cases   3 Abscess
                                           2 Misplaced Womb
                                           1 Cancer
                                           4 Torn cervix
                                           7 Prolapse
                                           2 Part of cervix removed
                                           5 Hysterectomy
                                           2 Tumour
                                           3 Ulceration of womb
                                           6 Unspecified
Various such as hernia, torn bladder, torn rectum, Cæsarian section—
"inflammation"   9 cases
Of the 77 altogether who have not had treatment (although 17 of
them have asked advice,)—
    33 are Backache cases, following on pregnancy
    4 have fallen uterus
    4 speak of "womb trouble"
    8 severe hæmorrhage
    6 have dysmenorrhœa
    1 has bad rectal pains
    8 have menorrhagia
    1 speaks of irritation of pelvis spreading to back passage
    12 simply say "severe pains in lower part of body" after birth of
      child

Income and Treatment

35   21 have had advice and followed it
with 4/- and under   of   2 have had advice and not followed it
per head per week   these   None use home remedies
"housekeeping" money   12 take no advice or remedy

76 with 4/1—6/- per head per week "housekeeping" money — of these:
- 46 have had advice and followed it
- 7 have had advice and not followed it
- 1 uses home remedies
- 22 take no advice or remedy

29 with 6/1—8/- per head per week "housekeeping" money — of these:
- 19 have had advice and followed it
- 4 have had advice and not followed it
- 1 uses home remedies
- 5 take no advice or remedy

27 with 8/1—10/- per head per week "housekeeping" money — of these:
- 10 have had advice and followed it
- 2 have had advice and not followed it
- 1 uses home remedies
- 14 take no advice or remedy

24 with over 10/- per head per week "housekeeping" money — of these:
- 18 have had advice and followed it
- 2 have had advice and not followed it
- None use home remedies
- 4 take no advice or remedy

7. BAD LEGS. 101 cases

(Varicose veins, ulcerated legs, white leg, phlebitis etc., but not legs merely described as aching.)

Average pregnancies. 6·5

28 in very bad houses

Income and Treatment

25 with 4/- and under per head per week "housekeeping" money — of these:
- 15 have had advice and followed it
- 4 have had advice and not followed it
- None use home remedies
- 6 take no advice or remedy

33 with 4/1—6/- per head per week "housekeeping" money — of these:
- 21 have had advice and followed it
- 4 have had advice and not followed it
- 4 use home remedies
- 4 take no advice or remedy

16 with 6/1—8/- per head per week "housekeeping" money — of these:
- 11 have had advice and followed it
- 2 have had advice and not followed it
- 1 uses home remedies
- 2 take no advice or remedy

11 with 8/1—10/- per head per week "housekeeping" money — of these:
- 8 have had advice and followed it
- None have had advice and not followed it
- None use home remedies
- 3 take no advice or remedy

16 with over 10/- per head per week "housekeeping" money — of these:
- 8 have had advice and followed it
- None have had advice and not followed it
- 5 use home remedies
- 3 take no advice or remedy

SUPPLEMENT TO CHAPTER III

Part of a letter from a District Nurse in an agricultural district. Dated February 1938.

. . . I know you are interested in things to do with the health of the people, and perhaps you would like to hear something of my work.

I am the Queen's District Nurse, Health Visitor and Midwife for six villages. I do general nursing, midwifery, tuberculosis visiting, health-visiting of children under 5, foster-children under 9 and am school nurse for five schools. So I really am concerned with my people from birth till 14 or 15 and then again when the girls become mothers.

My district extends 6 miles one way and 7 the other, and contains one Lighthouse, at which I have had one birth. The population is about 1900. I live in the biggest village. There is a good deal of forestry land and so I have a good many very isolated cottages, some nearly a mile off the road. But my faithful Austin 7 never seems to mind common, ploughed fields, or forest tracks, so I can generally get fairly near the cottage door. I will describe a rather typical day's work.

I try to do my midwifery cases first, but must fit them in so as to cover as little ground as possible.

8.30 I leave home; bath a mother and baby in village 1. 9.30 catch a babe of three months in its bath so can see it properly and weigh it without disturbing its sleep. 10. Bath another mother and babe in village 3, and go on to dress an old man's toe. Then to village 4, where I wash a girl with pneumonia and leave instructions about diet; she is beginning to get better, otherwise I should probably have gone to her first. Call in near by to persuade a mother to let her child have his tonsils removed; she says she doesn't mind, but Father won't hear of it; (it is always some-one who is not present who objects) I ask what time Father comes home,—5 o'cl.

On the way home I pay three visits to children under 5, put a poultice on a knee, and in my own village wash and dress a rheumatoid arthritis. She takes a long time so I leave her till last. I try to get my furthest away visits done altogether in the morning, so as to save petrol.

In the afternoon I may pay two ante-natal visits, and a T.B. report; a weekly visit to an old lady who lives alone; come in for a cup of tea and start out for evening visits about 5. I then see my mother and baby, visit the pneumonia case for temperature and to make her comfortable for the night. See Father about the tonsils, talk to him till I am hoarse and hope that I have convinced him that the operation is necessary; and so home to the writing of my reports.

Some days I get in more health visits and may do two sessions at a school inspection with the M.O.H. If anything is found wrong with a child, if the mother is not present, I call later on at the home and advise and help in any treatment, or urge hospital treatment.

We have no Welfare Centre or Ante-natal Clinic as the distances are too great. So I go to them in their homes instead. The sick, the well, ante- and post-natal all get home visits. I try to see all babies under a year once a month and weigh them; and the toddlers three or four times a year. Ante-natal at first once a month and then fortnightly and at the last weekly; post-natal when I am weighing the babies.

We make use of all the various health services here as far as possible; transport is our greatest difficulty, as the hospital for out-patients etc. and dental clinics for gas are 20 miles away – 1½ hours by bus – which means a whole day's outing. Most of the people pay into the hospital scheme 3d. a week for the family; in many cases the employer pays part of this. This covers all treatments at hospital, minor and major and teeth extractions; but transport costs a lot and a busy mother finds it often impossible to leave home for so long. They also mostly pay into the nursing association scheme, 1/1 a quarter, which covers my visits, or otherwise my visits cost 6d. each.

The children of school age come under the School medical services; the M.O.H. visits every school twice a year and every child has a routine inspection at 6, 9, and 13 years old. If anything is wrong, however slight, they are seen every 6 months, and the Mother, Teacher or myself can bring a child forward to be seen at any inspection for any complaint or anything out of the normal. And treatment or appliances such as glasses will if necessary be undertaken by the County Council and transport if necessary. The child can have one-third of a pint of milk for ½d. which is half-price; in some schools they provide Horlicks now instead of fresh milk, which is a pity I think.

The children under five and nursing and expectant mothers in big families can get 1 pint of milk per day for each of them. So I can in some cases get three pints a day for the family, which is a great help. It is very difficult to be sure that the mother drinks what is meant for her. They get it from their own milkman and the County Council pays for it. Cod Liver oil and Virol and dried milk are also provided for necessitous cases with a Doctor's Certificate. Fathers and children at work come under the National Health Insurance, but *very seldom* the mothers.

It is mother who gets left out so far as treatment goes. She can go to hospital for teeth and so on but she cannot afford transport nor as a rule the time, and no-one pays for transport for her, unless she is so ill as to need to go into the hospital as an in-patient. She *may* get the "family" doctor for herself as well as the children if she pays into the medical club 5/5 a quarter for herself and three or more children. If she does not pay in, she carries on as long as she possibly can without advice or treatment, and if I am visiting the house for one or more of her children, she thinks I can tell her all that is necessary. She will not start a doctor's bill for herself if she can possibly stand on her feet. Besides they don't really like having the doctor quite apart from the expense. They feel the doctor means giving way and that the business is more serious. And the doctor is a man and they know me better. Even in confinements they want me to carry on, and they all dread chloroform and beg me not to call the doctor in.

Nearly all the women have very bad teeth; they cannot afford going backwards and forwards to the dentist and cannot afford artificial ones. Enough fuss is made when a mother dies, but if they could pay more attention to teeth it would help matters a lot. Teeth, teeth, teeth, they are half the trouble, but the mothers don't believe it themselves.

I am afraid the children as a whole are rather pale and of poor physique. They have quantities of vegetables and bread; eggs when they are cheap and occasional rabbits; meat on Sundays. The good cooks make their own bread and rusks and bone stews and dumplings; but so many of them have poor breakfasts; tea and a shop cake and bread and butter to take with them to school for dinner and now the one-third of a pint of milk (or Horlick's !) They never have their windows open at night, for the rooms are small and draughty, and they have very few bed-clothes. I remember being called in suddenly for a confinement, and although I had seen the mother, (it was her first baby,) before and told her how to get things ready for me, she was lying on a bed without any bedclothes on it at all, and covered by her husband's coat. There was no water in the house and no clean basin for anything. I had to fetch everything and borrow bed-clothes. They go to bed much too late; this applies to the children particularly. They do not go to school if it is raining, for as a rule they have no macintoshes and only one pair of boots.

I find the best time to talk to the mothers is when I am bathing her baby; we go in every day for a fortnight after the birth; it is so much easier to tell her things gradually and talk things out together; we can do a lot with a young mother and she is generally very anxious to learn.

I find them all wonderfully friendly and so pleased with a visit; even if they have no intention of taking my advice they generally seem to want me to come and soon tell me if they think I have left them too long without a visit. It is wonderful how one finds out, and without asking, their joys and troubles, all their aches and pains, all their hopes and family histories; they expect advice about baby's rash; what to do with Granny; Father's false teeth; Johnny's boots which *will* wear out; teach Father to make a custard, a milk pudding, barley water; how to cure a rough skin; falling hair; Lily's love affairs; the pump is out of order; rain comes into the bedroom; a pattern for a vest; improvise a cot for the new babe; show Mary how to knit herself a new jumper . . . and so on and so on. I sometimes wonder what my job really is, but it is all intensely interesting, and now I have been here seven years and feel as if I had known them all my life. . . . I am no good at letter writing, but I hope this will interest you and answer your question as to what I really do ! . . .

CHAPTER IV

THE ATTITUDE TO LIFE AND HEALTH

"THE constant struggle with poverty this last four years has made me feel very nervy and irritable and this affects my children. I fear I have not the patience that good health generally brings. When I am especially worried about anything I feel as if I have been engaged in some terrific physical struggle and go utterly limp and for some time unable to move or even think coherently. This effect of mental strain expressed in physical results seems most curious and I am at a loss to properly explain it to a doctor."

This is from the wife of an unemployed man in Essex. She was a book-keeper shorthand-typist before marriage and is obviously better educated than the majority of the 1,250. Hence probably her greater capacity both to express herself and to realize the effects of the "constant struggle".

Her words give a significant summary of what is undoubtedly the physical and mental condition of a very large number of the women, even when they do not specify particular diseases, and claim a general feeling of well-being. There is evidence in hundreds of cases either of a grim and tacit acceptance of this sort of condition, or of so low a standard of good-health that in spite of this physical weariness and emotional tension resulting often in sleeplessness and constant headaches, anaemia etc. they do not feel justified in giving any answer but "yes" to the first question, "Do you generally feel fit and well". Tiredness and strain are considered the lesser inevitable inconveniences of marriage and of a growing family, and must be accepted with the same resignation as getting old. For instance, Mrs. A.R.S. of Cardiff, says:—"With regard to the difference before and after marriage. I do not think there is any that progressing years would not account for. I find one complaint which is more prevalent than formerly and that is headaches. No doubt this is due to the care of a growing and boistrous family. Giddiness and nerves also attack me now, and when the latter becomes too acute I find the prescriptions of my doctor of great benefit. The greatest difference now and before marriage is undoubtedly tired and aching feet. They are frequently a cause of great discomfort at the end of the day. The cause you will readily understand to be the long hours it is necessary for me to be about. Subject to the foregoing my general health and appetite is quite good and subject to the whims of the baby my sleep is very sound".

This woman is the wife of an employed machine minder. She is 40, has four children well-spaced, (the Essex woman has only three, equally well-spaced) and after the deduction of rent has £1 19s. 0d. for "house-keeping". She too was a clerk before marriage. She says she feels "usually fit and well", but she has constant headaches, giddiness and lassitude, (all of which have been bad enough to justify consulting a doctor) nerves and aching legs. In her opinion these however are not worth really worrying about, and in contrast to the Essex woman, she is cheerful and happy. Compared to the majority of the 1,250, the circumstances of these two women are *not* particularly hard. The first lives in the country, has a good garden and a diet made up to good by the inclusion of eggs and vegetables from her own garden, and she gets a certain amount of rest in the day. She is poor, and terribly worried by her husband's unemployment, and has been used to a standard of health and material surroundings before marriage to which she cannot attain now. She says, inter alia, "Never having been trained to housework, I find it very difficult to run my home efficiently, very small allowance prevents purchase of many labour saving devices." She does not feel fit and well, and indeed it is clear that she has had severe post-natal trouble, is very anæmic, which she thinks is the cause of extremely bad teeth, (which she has extracted "usually, when quite unbearable") bad feet for which she puts boracic in her stockings, and excruciating headaches, due to the anæmia.

The Cardiff woman has a very good house, and no complaints to make about it. Her diet is good, except that she has not followed the doctor's advice to have more fish and less meat for her giddiness. There is in these two cases no apparent reason that they should not be in better health than they are, except that their standard is low, and that they accept, one grudgingly and with bitterness, the other cheerfully, their condition as inherent in the lives they have to lead.

There is absolutely no evidence of hypochondria. Three or four out of the hundreds who have said that they don't feel well have failed to produce any ailments, or any direct evidence of ill-health. But even these are living under conditions which would very easily account for an enduring sense of strain and overwork, one of the results of which is the inability to think about health or to notice any particular physical condition. For instance Mrs. L. of East London says that she does not feel fit and well; she is laconic in all her answers, but gives no ailments and no difficulties about her house and home. She does not find her day's work too hard; but she has no leisure and an extremely poor diet. She has had eight children, of whom two have died, and she has 35/- a week for "housekeeping" including rent; *and the whole family (eight) is living in one room*. No-one would accuse her of being an impostor on the subject of health, even though she does not admit to feeling well ! It might perhaps be said that Mrs. R. of Battersea is unnecessarily disgruntled at the size of her family. She is 32 and has three children, very well spaced and is "expecting again". But she says she only feels "fair", and puts down as her ailment "Too frequent child-bearing which has lowered my vitality". She is however, very poor and lives in a bad house, of which she lets out two rooms. She was a nursemaid before marriage, wherein perhaps lies the explanation ! She is the only case in which it may be felt that there is *any* exaggeration of difficulties and bad health.

The outstanding feature of the woman's attitude to health, (especially to her own, but quite often to that of her family as well, when, through some casual observation, light is shed on this) is her confident assertion of physical well-being, typified by such answers to the first question as "Yes", "Pretty good", "Usually", in spite of the long list of ailments which follows. She even becomes apologetic if she feels that this answer must be qualified. For instance one woman in Caerphilly answers this question, "Yes, until of late", and says "I get very bad turns of faintness and very giddiness and get very fagged with least exursion," and later on takes care to explain that her husband is delicate, that she has consulted Dr. P. about her faintness, and "he stated blood-pressure, so I mustn't complain".[1] Another woman at Saffron Walden says she does "*not always*" feel fit and well; she is very anæmic and rheumatic, but says she consulted the doctor "only because the monthly strain became far too much, so perhaps I shouldn't mention this".

For many of them, good health is any interval between illnesses, or at the best the absence of any *incapacitating* ailment. They consider themselves not only fortunate, but well, as long as they can keep going and can get through the work which must be done. One woman rather pathetically recognises that her criterion is fallacious, by saying that she usually feels fit and well, "in the sense that one is not laid up, and is able to carry on with the work cheerfully". She is an intelligent, keen woman, living in London, and comparatively well off. Her husband does jobbing work with his own motor van. She has had five pregnancies, including one miscarriage, and one baby died. She has been very anæmic since the miscarriage

[1] This woman is quoted again in the chapter on Diet; pp. 166 and 178.

eight years ago, and has varicose veins which she "thinks
are hereditary". But she has not consulted any doctor
about these, and only occasionally sought advice "when
feeling very nervy". The visitor says that "This mother
is always keen to ask questions on health even troubling
to write them down to remember to ask", and she has
been a regular attendant at the Infant Welfare Centre,
and is untiring in her devotion to and care of the children,
never going out in the evening unless a friend can come
in to watch over the children, and taking them often to
the park, which is rather a long way off. Again Mrs. G.
of Cardiff is 37, has seven children all under thirteen and
says she feels fit and well. She has kidney trouble for which,
on the advice of the Ante-natal Clinic she takes barley
water and lemon; and constant headaches which she
thinks are entirely due to "defective vision" and for which
she wears glasses. No other ailments are mentioned in
this part of the enquiry. But under special difficulties
about home and housework she says "kneeling since birth
of baby. Phebitis (sic) with ulceration unable to bear
weight of body on same." And there is Mrs. P. of Glasgow,
(Glasgow seems to abound in buoyant, intelligent, and
infinitely energetic women!) whose indomitable spirit is
shown in every answer. She is 46, and has had five children
born alive, one miscarriage and one still-birth. Two children
have died. The family live in a tenement house, in one
room and a kitchen for which she pays 9/– out of a total
allowance of 40/–. (Her husband pays for clothing for the
family in addition to this). Under the drawbacks of her
house she says "Outside lavatory, (used by six families.)
Public house at close which is objectionable owing to
disgusting habits of men and bad language. House too
small; no difficulties otherwise, except smell of beer worst
in summer." Three of her children (she does not mention
whether the two dead ones are included in this) have been
in the T.B. hospital for six months, and a convalescent
home for six months; these also attended T.B. Dispensary

regularly. One boy has been operated on for appendicitis. She is a very good mother, (in spite of this rather alarming evidence to the contrary); she attends regularly V.A.D. and Public Health classes; holds a certificate for First Aid and Home Nursing, and got second prize in "care of children"! As to her own state of health, she says that she feels quite well and fit except for hernia (umbilical), caused by child-bearing. She has had one operation for this five years ago, and is waiting for another. She had a Cæsarian section also five years ago (this was her youngest child, who has T.B.), and she has been sterilised. She broke her ankle a short while ago, but that is all right now; she apologised for speaking of the hernia to the visitor as a complaint, and has had no holiday whatever for nine years.

Such cases can be multiplied over and over again. They do not show any lack of intelligence or of realization that there is such a possibility as good health, because the care they take of their children, (although as in the case of the Glasgow woman it may be a discouraging fight) indicates that for the family at least they have a positive standard of fitness. While acknowledging the courage of this attitude, one cannot help sometimes feeling rather impatient at the failure to put into practice for themselves the knowledge which they have taken so much trouble to acquire on behalf of their children about health in general. Here is Mrs. V. of Bolton. The Visitor describes her as a "quick lively little woman, a good manager and cook, and intelligent about her own health". She is 48, a widow, with three children, who all lived at home till recently, when the son, who was unemployed, went to London to look for work. She lives rent free with coal and light free in return for the caretaking of a Church House. Her housekeeping money consists of the wages of her two girls aged 17 and 14, which amount to £1 a week and her pension of 10/-. She might now be taking things easy a bit. She says she does "not always feel fit and well". She has had neuritis for fifteen years, owing she thinks to two very bad falls. The doctor told her to keep the parts warm, so she used thermogene wool, but nothing else. She has had rheumatism "real bad" for a few years, owing to "doing too much washing and cleaning with water". For this she has started to take Kalzana tablets; the doctor says she "ought to do less work and washing, but I can't always manage". She has had chronic mastitis in the breast for ten years, and she goes occasionally to the doctor "to see if the lumps have got any bigger; his advice is to leave well alone". She has had a displaced bowel for "a few years" and has been told to take care and not do lifting or heavy washing, "I don't seem to be able to manage this." She says that her son being away, she now has to shovel and carry coke for the boiler of the Church House, "which is rather hard work for a woman," and though she tries about her day's work, "to averige it out, wash days and social days in club are very hard days". And she adds on the back of her form:—"I also suffer from stomach troubles which take the form of gastritis the doctor give me some medicine for the trouble and I have to be a bit careful what I eat. I have also got a tired heart which the doctor says will not do its work properly. I blame the cause of that through nursing first my mother through years of indifferent health and then nursing my husband owing to him having a stroke and being completely helpless for eight weeks, during which time I had to lift him and I think I over-strained my heart, and now the least bit of extra work such as mounting inclines (!) or stairs lifting buckets etc. makes me feel dreadfully tired and only treatment for it the doctor says is going easy and resting when able to do so, but can't manage much." She then describes in detail the two very bad falls she had, the second one when "I injured the tail of my spine and it has not been proper better since it effects my back and brings a pain right up to my shoulders when I do a lot of sweeping or long mopping or kneading bread. I have had an inflamed gall bladder the doctor

advice was to stay in bed and keep warm, but that I can't."
She is obviously not going to let up at all, and although
she seems to have implicit faith in her doctor, she does
not go so far as to take his advice. And why knead bread?

And another example of disregard, largely unnecessary,
of the doctor's advice comes from Mrs. C. from Essex.
She is 42. She goes to the Welfare Centre and has talks
with the Health Visitor. She has only three children and
the youngest is 12½. She has had one miscarriage. Her
cottage is very damp and old, and the drain from three
other houses is in the middle of the back-yard. She has
no cooking stove but only an open fireplace on which to
cook. So it is clear that her circumstances are not comfortable nor her work easy. But she goes out to work two
hours daily. She does not feel well; she has had pains
in her back for twelve years (since her last confinement)
for which the doctor "advises a pessary and probably an
operation"; rheumatism owing to the dampness of the
house, for which her doctor gives her an embrocation
"when the pain acute"; constipation through lack of
time for regularity, for which she takes syrup of figs and
castor oil; (nurse says she must "alter her diet, have more
walking exercise and regular habits"); and floodings due
to heavy work probably and not much real rest. Nurse
advises "visit the doctor". Mrs. C. has bracketed all these
together and remarks laconically "Money not plentiful
enough". The Health Visitor says:— "This woman is
always at work either in her own home or assisting some
neighbour in trouble apart from her paid outside work.
She has been repeatedly advised to have an operation
but has a horror of hospitals but sometimes says laughingly
that she will go to hospital when her youngest daughter
leaves school".

The acceptance of a low standard of health, or the
neglect of conditions which might be improved is not
always due to the deliberate refusal through poverty,
hardwork or maternal unselfishness which are exemplified

by most of the women quoted above, but may be caused also either by stupidity and ignorance, (in which case the family suffers as well,) or by the wearing down of the spirit.

An elderly woman in Derby suffers from bad neuralgia, for which the doctor advised the extraction of all her teeth; the remedy she takes is strong tea ! She has bad rheumatism for which she merely rubs herself; mental depression for which she says there is no remedy; and headaches which she caused by bad eyesight for which she wears spectacles from Woolworth's because the Doctor advised spectacles. She has had nine children of whom only one is living, and two miscarriages. She lives alone with her husband,—an unemployed labourer, complains that her house is extremely inconvenient, and that her work is too hard for her. But she has money enough for a fair diet, and frequent visits to the pictures and the public house.

Devonshire seems to produce unenterprising although very hard-working mothers. Three of them from near Exeter are aged 32, 35 and 35 respectively and have had nine, seven and eight pregnancies. They are very poor, work very hard, and bring up all their children in what the Health Visitor calls a "pale anæmic way." They all need "new teeth" but cannot afford them, and in consequence they all have indigestion, because they cannot "chew proper". The woman with nine living children, who is 32 has been to the Birth Control Clinic in Exeter, where the doctor told her that her "womb was twisted over". She leaves it at that, and is doing nothing more about it, though it gives her bad backache.

In most of the young mothers there is hopefulness and optimism expressed in every line, but one is forced to the opinion, by comparing these with the women in the early thirties who obviously started equally cheerfully on their married life, that as the years go on, one after another of the positive benefits, sources of enjoyment, and opportunities for general well-being and happiness will be lost in the increasing worry, work and responsibilities of a growing family with whom the income always fails to keep pace. The change in the woman's outlook is so subtle, and she becomes so mentally choked by the pressure of work, that often she either is not aware herself of the lowering of the standards with which she started, or consciously resigns herself to it without apparent regret, and merely turns her thoughts, if she manages to keep the remnants of her original optimism, to the future, when the children will be grown up and she will again have a little peace of mind and time and opportunity to rest. Mrs. S. of London, does not complain much of her health, only of nerves, and "just headaches, weakness, lassitude", all due to "worry through periods of unemployment and getting into debt with money lenders". She is 40, has been married 20 years and has eleven children. (She had written thirteen and then corrected it to eleven, adding that she has had no miscarriages or still-births; it is quite possible therefore that she has had thirteen children of whom two have died). Her children all live at home except one, so that there is a family of twelve in four rooms. Her husband is a carpenter. She adds, "Please note we have had a rather trying time especially when unemployed and have had to make sacrifices in the interest of the children, who arrived more quickly than I could cope with. Matters are not so hard now that the children are growing and are helping a little towards the income, although my husband's occupation is not regular, and the most trying times is giving (? going) the six day waiting period on the unemployment benefit one has no alternative but to borrow for this as we cannot save owing to the uncertainty of work in the building trade, of course we are trusting that we shall all three (this appears to mean her husband and the eldest boy and girl, aged 19 and 17 respectively) stay working, then we shall be happy !" When "all" are working, her total for housekeeping is £5 out of which she pays 16/1 rent.

Mrs. L. C. of Cardiff, says she has been ailing since marriage. She was a housemaid in private service before and was never ill. She is now 39. She has had six children (all still living at home) and one miscarriage; she has a fair house but no bathroom or hot water, which she misses "sadly". She is badly constipated and has piles and has had bad backache "ever since her first confinement which was a difficult one". She now has also palpitation and cardiac pains. For none of these has she consulted anyone, but she listens to the wireless talks on health. She makes no complaints and after her remark about the lack of hot water and a bathroom she says hopefully "things will ease up a bit soon when the children grow older". She is however only 39 and her two youngest children are 4 and 3 !

Mrs. L. of Bromley, Kent, says she has not felt well since marriage; she too was in private service before marriage, and says she was never ill. She married at 21 and is now 37. She has six children, all under 15. She had a bad fall during her second pregnancy for which she did not get advice, "as I was too busy with the baby, and didn't think it much". It resulted, however, in a tuberculous rib, which had to be removed, and since then she has had general debility, and has been extremely rheumatic. Her husband is tubercular, and she remarks "No time for my own ailments which I have got used to now". Even the Health Visitor remarks "She has no domestic troubles and her husband is quite good to her and considerate. We have sent her away for two years running to help her to recoup and she is going away this summer. Personally I think her ill health is mostly due to insufficient nourishment."

"Ease up a bit soon" . . . Too often by the time the children are grown up, the woman is worn out. Mrs. H. of Battersea is 54. She has had sixteen pregnancies including two still-births and one miscarriage. Her husband is unemployed so she must go out to work a little, and she earns on an average 2/6 a week. She has only three children living at home now, of whom the youngest is 9. She says in answer to the first question, "Never two days alike", and to the enquiry "Is your day's work too hard for you", she says, "Sometimes it is and sometimes it isn't it is what sort of trouble you make of it;" and about difficulties "Nothing to complain of got to be done so just get on with it and do whatever there is to be done." She is very rheumatic and has been to St. Thomas's Hospital for treatment; "he gave me medicin and oitment but afraid he can't cure me quite of it". The doctor says she ought to wear glasses, but she can't afford these. Her diet is atrocious, and she remarks that she eats either nothing or "just anything I can get when I have the money to buy it with." There does not seem much chance of easing up for her in the near future.

Another good example of the comparatively easy time coming too late is found in Mrs. W. of Smethwick. She is 50, has had five children and one stillborn. She was in domestic service before marriage, and married at 22. Her husband is a wages clerk, and now that her children are earning they are quite well off as compared with most of the families under review: £5 a week, and they are buying their new house on instalments. But she complains wearily of neuralgia, "worse the last two years", headache and "very, very tired", all due she says to "Anxiety of rearing the family of five children income being too small to met all the needs while they were young going out to work to help to maintain them and educate them." These are the ailments she seems to notice most and are the only ones mentioned in the answer to the second question; but further on she says she has had to consult the family doctor about rheumatic troubles and to go to hospital for "one Prolapsis three years ago". Of an unhappy elderly woman outside Derby, the visitor writes "This woman is very miserable; she has no leisure occupation and cannot read or write. She cannot go out much as her leg is too bad; she only goes to the shops once a week when well enough". She suffers from nerves, headaches (due to the worry of husband's unemployment,)—general debility and shortness of breath, and a very bad ulcerated leg. "Her leg has been bad for over twenty years; for two years she went three times a week to the Infirmary for treatment (10 miles distant) but had to stop two years ago owing to husband's unemployment; she said the lotion obtained at the Infirmary did much to ease the intolerable pain, but she cannot now afford the fares (1/-) or the lotion. The ulcers have now burst." She has had eight children; only one, a son of 23 now lives at home. "He is a brass-glazer and a big man, requiring adequate food. He gets it,—the old people do not."

And lastly another old woman, Mrs. D. of Scarborough. She is 69 and "never" feels well. She has had a displaced womb for 43 years. She has had three living children and nine miscarriages. She says she had "unnatural labour" with the first child; and from then "every $4\frac{1}{2}$ months had a miscarriage; had two children and six miscarriages in four years." She has always had bladder trouble, and now for years has suffered acutely from rheumatoid arthritis, inflammation of the nerves and constipation. For years she consulted a herbalist, to whom she paid 9/- a fortnight. Six years ago she went to Newcastle to consult a doctor about her bladder trouble and he found a growth "but too dangerous to operate". She has had bad shingles. She still puts her faith in herbal treatment, but says she "must make the best of it all now."

These two last women are of the generation for which *no* welfare centres or other sources of health teaching or advice were provided when they were young married women. (Mrs. D. left school at 11 and worked for 1/6 a week). But in spite of the knowledge and help which the Welfare Centres give now to the mothers of young children, which is acknowledged with enthusiasm and gratitude over and over again in the answers of these

women, the mother continues to neglect her own health
to such an appalling degree that one wonders how many
of them will be able to enjoy the comparative rest which
later life is bound to bring. The writer of this report was
speaking to an elderly bed-ridden woman in a country
village a short while ago. She lives in a cottage by herself,
but her married daughter who lives near spends a long time
every day looking after her, and is constantly in and out;
(an extra burden for the daughter, who has six small
children of her own, and is the wife of an agricultural
labourer earning 33/- a week). The old lady has rheumatoid
arthritis, and is very small and weak. The writer asked
her whether she was able to enjoy her rest, and the care
her daughter now took of her, to which she replied; "Oh
my dear if I could have had a little of it twenty years ago,
it would have saved a great deal of this", and she held
out her hands, which as she put it are all "housened up".
Her husband was a sea captain, and she used to go every
voyage with him, (her room is hung with the pictures of
all his ships). She had nine children, and often would
have five at a time on the ship. She was asked if she had
had any trouble with her own health in the actual business
of child-bearing, at which she became rather embarrassed
and said, "That's as may be; we dursn't fash with them
things, but they were all bonny chillun".

Some of the younger women show that in the early
years of marriage they make great efforts to take care of
themselves, realizing, a little vaguely perhaps, that not
only for their own and their husbands' sakes it was
desirable to keep well, but for that of the unborn children
also. They learn eagerly from whatever source they can,
particularly from the Welfare Centres or District Nurse
with whom, as the children arrive, they are in regular touch.
Some of them do gymnastic exercises, spend as much time
as possible out of doors, go early to bed and get up early
(the most frequently mentioned dictum of health) read
books and papers on health, and listen to the wireless.

Even when faced soon after marriage with the spectre of unemployment, they show or showed a keen interest in running their home carefully and scientifically and do not neglect even themselves. Mrs. B. of Blackburn, (whose budget is quoted in full on p. 171) is a good sample of this. She is 23, and has been married four years and has one child of 3 and another on the way. Her husband is unemployed and she has 10/- a week to spend on food for the three of them. She goes out from 2 till 5 with the child, "because fresh air so important for both" and it "helps" her headaches. She goes regularly to the Clinic, "where they tell you a little". It is obvious that she laps up the "little" with avidity. Then there is a young woman in Rochdale, Mrs. R. aged 22. She has been married seven years ! She says, "I was married very young at the age of 15 years my mother died when I was 13 years. So I really had no-one to tell me enything. Still I do not regret having been married. I have two lovly childern the boy off which has won two baby shows one resently. They are both healthy childern and like myself have not had eny bad health. I have consulted the clinic when enything as been the matter such as colds and have found them great help as I think Clinics are a fine thing for young or old mothers, and also for enyone in need of enything such as cough mixture or Powders which are both good things also for the Doctor and Nurses advice they really look after your health and Babys." And another young woman in Hampstead remarks "One learns a lot when visiting Clinics with their baby and the various visiting nurses and such people". She is 36, has been married six years and only has one child. Another in Coventry, aged 26 with one child of 3 spends five hours in the park on fine days, with her baby, and takes books from the Public library on health and also books about babies "as I am very interested in child welfare" and attends Clinics.

Sometimes, but not often, the young woman makes a

bad start. This may be due to bad health, (mostly anæmia) before marriage, or to stupidity which results in no wish to learn either for herself or for her children. Two bad examples come from Llanelly. Mrs. R. says she is depressed, rundown and very tired. She has always suffered from constipation and catarrh. For none of these has she consulted anyone. She has three children already, (she is 24 and has been married five years) and says she "always has to stay in the house as the children are so young". She is in a Council house and the only complaint she makes about it is that she has to cook on an electric cooker, as there is no ordinary oven ! She does not take her children to the Clinic, and is bored and tired with her day's work. And Mrs. J. of the same town is 25 and has three children. She lives in a slum house, and the kitchen is full of mice, but she says there are no difficulties about her housework. She suffers from "Bad chest" which she says is caused by the dampness of her house,—and for which the "Doctor told me not to overdo myself with housework." This presumably explains the fact that she gets up at 10 a.m ! She also has headache, faintness, and constipation for which she has consulted no-one, nor taken any remedy. Her diet is atrocious. The visitor writes "She is a most improvident young woman;—the rare type which *makes* a slum."

And in Rochdale, Mrs. F. aged 24 with one child, lives in a back-to-back house, "infested with bugs, fleas and beetles". She has bad gastritis owing, so the Health Visitor says, to very bad teeth. She had three teeth removed just before the baby was born; and has been continually advised to clean her teeth and to have more out,—advised by husband, Clinic Doctor and Nurse, but "she is very obstinate. She dawdles about her housework and never appears to be tidy or finished, and consequently hasn't much leisure though she hasn't a lot to do. She did not attend the Ante-natal Clinic till the 8th month, and does not put into practice any of the advice given her." Another

1 "The abiding maternal personality." [*Edith Tudor Hart*

[Edith Tudor Hart

2 The typical afternoon "rest."

3 The waiting-room of a large hospital.

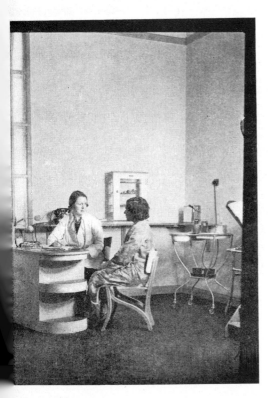

4 "At the Clinic, the mother finds the atmosphere is easier and pleasanter; very often the consultant is a woman like herself, and will meet her half-way in the recital of her grievances". (p. 55)

[*Edith Tudor Hart*

[*Edith Tudor Hart*

5 " The travelling Clinic of the country ".

[*Edith Tudor Hart*

6 " I think the Clinics are a fine thing for young or old mothers and also for anyone in need of anything." (p. 83)

7 "Taken as a whole, their vitality must be prodigious, for in spite of every embarrassment, life goes on undiminished in bulk." (p. 95)

Edith Tudor Hart]

8, 9, 10 Fronts, backs, interiors of the Victorian family houses now converted into tenements.

Housing Centre Photos)

11, 12 A pair of Essex cottages before and after reconditioning by the County Council.

13 "Where we learn
different ways of
living and making
best of all articles,
and best ways of
living." (p. 90)

14 The Community
Centre in a new
block of flats in
W London.

young mother of nineteen years lives in a slum court in Derby; (the whole court is condemned). She suffers from hysteria and nervous debility which came on four months after the birth of the baby; she also has very bad backache, of which she does not know the cause, and for which she rubs her back with liniment. She says she very rarely goes out of the house, but "sometimes goes to the recreation ground with baby". She finds that "baby and housework occupies all my time; house needs constant tidying, dirty walls and damp and paper comes off". She has no copper, no sink, no-where to keep coal. She does not go to the Clinic even for her baby.

Such cases however are rare. There is a much larger number of women at the other end of the scale who, with every sort of ill-health to contend with, generally with large families to look after, and probably some major disaster to aggravate their difficulties, make a steady untiring effort to keep themselves as fit as they possibly can. They take advantage of every opportunity for advice and treatment, plan out their day methodically and carefully so that though all their work gets done, they manage to get a little rest and know how to keep always to their programme, unless some unforeseen disaster occurs. There is no lack of such women, but as far as can be judged from this investigation they are to be found far more frequently in the north of England and in Scotland than in the south ! The Glasgow woman already quoted (on p. 73) is a fair example of a courageous fight for an ailing family, but she is obviously a robust woman, physically as well as mentally, and she *feels well enough* to cope with her difficulties. Here on the other hand is a woman from Durham, the wife of a miner (employed). She is quite definite about her complaints both as regards her house and her own health. The Health Visitor describes her as "an amazing woman, with indomitable pluck; she has been delicate all her life, and is extremely careful to preserve though without undue fussing whatever strength and health remains for her. Her children are splendid, her husband devoted to her." She is only 32, has been married fifteen years and has seven children the eldest of whom is 14. She lives in a colliery house; it has an open ash-privy at the back; the back bedroom is damp and the rain comes in; the kitchen ceiling is unsafe; there is no sink under the tap; the coal house and ash-pit are at the end of a long garden and coal and ashes have to be carried through the sitting room which is used as a bedroom. *The ground floor windows do not open.* In her spare time (!) she makes mats, for which she gets given clothes in return. She gets up at 4 a.m. and goes to bed at any time between 10 and midnight. She "sometimes" goes back to bed again after 4. She does her own baking at home, and the diet given is miraculous. She drinks a lot of water, and they get a lot of green vegetables from their own garden, including lettuce daily in summer. Her husband helps her with the heavy work when he is at home, such as carrying coals and lifting heavy pans on to an open fire. None of the children have ever been to hospital or needed outside treatment. She consults the Health Visitor, the District nurse and the colliery doctor, and all sickness has been nursed in the home. Now these are her own ailments. (1) Neuritis; from which she has suffered for two years owing, in her opinion, to getting wet, the heavy work of "possing", mangling etc. She rubs her shoulder with oils and puts on hot flannels, on the advice of the colliery doctor. (2) Pyorrhœa; on the advice of the colliery doctor she has had all her teeth extracted; (3) Kidney trouble, due to Bright's disease at 5 years; she takes medicine for this; (4) headaches and biliousness; life-long, due to the kidney trouble; she takes tablets for this; (5) Cystitis during her last pregnancy due to getting wet, and heavy work; for this she rested in bed and kept warm; (6) Pain in right side at menstrual periods, due to ovarian trouble; the colliery doctor gives medicine for this by which "he hopes to avoid an operation." Mrs. H. of Sheffield is another courageous woman. She is 37, has 36/6 for everything including rent and pays 8/6 for a poor house in an industrial district. The visitor writes: "She has experienced worry due to illness and occasional financial difficulties all her married life . . . in 1921 at the time of the General Strike the first baby was born. Her husband was unemployed and during the whole period of pregnancy she was unable to have sufficient nourishment and lived almost entirely on bread and tea. When the child was born it weighed only 4lbs. and has always been an invalid, suffering from endocarditis and very bad rheumatism. The mother was in a very run-down condition and nine months later had a miscarriage. She has never been away for a holiday since her marriage and has constantly been in an environment of sickness. She has been very sensible, and looked after her own health as far as possible. She has good glasses and a good set of false teeth. She keeps quite well physically but suffers mentally. She realizes her daughter will never be well and strong and this causes mental depression, against which she is constantly fighting. Her husband has had gastritis for twelve years and both he and the daughter have a special diet. This is expensive and the wife has to sacrifice herself. She sleeps with her daughter and never has a good night's rest."

The Rotherham woman with an invalid son, quoted a little later on (p. 92) is another example of courage,—although as far as her own health is concerned she is obviously sceptical, but not unintelligent.

And here is another woman from Rotherham. She is 33, has been married 14 years and has had eight children of whom two have died. *She has only one leg*, having had the other amputated at the age of 13. She says her greatest difficulty is the "big washings on account of family, find the work very hard having only one leg. Cannot feed and clothe properly husband and children on means test. Try to pay a little each week for clothing, just re-housed and have back rent to pay off weekly money." She suffers from headaches, bad constipation, indigestion and dizziness. She goes regularly to the Ante-natal and Child Welfare Clinics, and gets extra milk. She has subscribed regularly to Health Clubs and Hospital insurance schemes and has been to hospital for treatment once for mastitis and once for septic poisoning in her fingers. She says "Try as I can, it is impossible to get better than I am, not able to get proper meals at proper times and then eating too quickly, and the hardness of the work." She takes Beecham's pills, Epsom Salts and MacLean's stomach powders, though these "not doctor's recommendations, but then can't do as he says." She gets no leisure except occasionally to "go and see mother and play whist, have been to pictures twice in last 2 years."

But the South also can produce its courageous and upstanding women. Mrs. R. of Cardiff has five children under 9 and the eldest, a boy, has only one leg, which complicates her work. She is cheerful and a good manager. Her own account of her life is quoted on p. 120.

As to health-teaching, as has been shown before, about one-third of the women say firmly that they have had none, and merely use their common sense. Another 10% rely on the very elementary rules they learnt at school or from their mothers. This appears generally to mean that as long as the family is what the mother calls well, and as long as she is "keeping things going" all right, she does not concern herself with her health, or seek any knowledge. To her the positive state about which something must be done is *being ill*, and it does not occur to her that by the introduction into the routine of her life of a little additional care or science, she might prolong this normal condition of not being ill, or even build it into something better. As her knowledge is so sketchy, (how indeed can it be otherwise, as long as no teaching on this subject is a compulsory part of her equipment either at school or as a young woman ?) she will have the haziest idea of where to draw the line between good and bad health. A woman in

Birmingham says she has had no teaching, "other than we have a fair knowledge how to keep well through experience, keeping reasonable hours, teetotal, and living moderately with good plain food." This woman consults a doctor "sometimes when things are not all right" but for the most part a "John Bull" book, or "Home doctor", which she finds "useful". "Commonsense the best guide" is the answer given over and over again to the question on health education; or, "all through experience", or "through my own mind", or sometimes regretfully such as "None; owing to large family have very little time to spare for going to Welfare Centre and early bed make night classes impossible." A good many mention breathing exercises as the sum total of their health teaching, and evidently still perform these rites with religious regularity, "as we were told it was good for us"; (evidently no other explanation was offered). A few women have got very definite home-made theories about health, probably derived from an extremely sensible up-bringing, but without any scientific teaching or reading to back it up. For instance there is a country widow aged 47, with four healthy children : she says "I have always from birth been used to living a regular life viz a good walk every day, plenty of fruit and vegetables and milk. Have never touched beer stout or spirits and only on very rare occasions have a cigarette and very much against the use of artificial make-up depending on nature. Haven't time to trouble about own little aches and pains with four little ones to be Father and Mother to. Plenty of exercise and walking are the best medicine for the health and plain fresh well-cooked food instead of so much tinned stuff and a good old-fashioned suet pudding in the winter. Onions I never miss a day without having some of that much dispised vegetabl e and would rather go without my tea than miss my onions which can also save serious illnesses if sliced and put in a piece of muslin and make into a poultice similar to linseed and used the same way."

Although as has been pointed out a good many of the younger women seem to seek out means of learning about health and eagerly assimilate any literature, talks or lectures which they can find on the subject, such women do not amount to more than 10% of the whole, and when once the family has grown to more than two or three in number, very few mothers are able to make any real study of health by reading scientific or quasi-scientific books, attending lectures etc. etc. There is the woman in Glasgow already quoted who took a prize in the care of children. And another woman mentions that she is very much interested in Child Welfare and attends classes. She was a school teacher before marriage, and would know where to look for the information that she needs. In a few places there are Community centres or Clubs, which partly fulfil this need; classes are held in domestic routine and practical household methods. For instance in Caerphilly there is a "Community house for Ladies at Senghenydd where we learn different ways of living and making best of all articles and best ways of living." Two ladies in Caerphilly mention this Club with appreciation. The rather complacent lady in Rotherham, who is quoted on p. 112 of the next chapter belongs to a "Keep fit class" and the "Fellowship of Marriage", and enjoys "healthful discussions, which broaden the outlook and improve the mind."

As to the degree of ill-health which must be reached before the mother asks advice for herself, and the further stage at which the advice is taken, it has already been shown that owing first to poverty, then to the weight of other cares and to the arduousness of their work, the great majority of these women postpone seeking advice and treatment till the last possible moment. There is, besides the pressure of every day life, a good deal of scepticism about the efficacy of a doctor's remedies. A doctor cannot get employment for the husband, and unemployment is put down over and over again as the real cause of the wife's illness. "Husband's work the only cure"; "no remedy but employment". What is the use of spending money and time on a doctor in these circumstances? Toothache, rheumatism, faintness are all sometimes put down to worry, through unemployment. In one case a "bad discharge from the eyes" is due to husband's unemployment. Another describes the effect on herself of her husband finding work after a long period of unemployment; "I have been married twelve years and out of that my husband has been out of work through ill health and unemployment for seven years. He has been working for 2 years now and oh, if it only continues we are getting turned round. It makes me feel quite different." One woman speaks of a "sinking feeling in stomach during unemployment period," and says "Husband seeking remedy daily", (under remedy for ailments.) An unemployed labourer's wife in Essex, who has very bad health and six children, says the cause of everything is "being runned down through worry", and asks no advice.

When a condition gets too bad, medical advice must be sought, but that it is received with an attitude of polite scepticism, terror or despair is evident in hundreds of the cases. Over and over again operations are advised but the woman cannot think of leaving her home, or is too frightened by the suggestion. A woman in Accrington, aged 36 with five children, says she has frequent head pains, which she thinks are due to having had St. Vitus' dance at the age of 12. She hasn't "mentioned the fact to a doctor or a clinic". She also has frequent pains in right arm and right side of body and lump under arm"; she was operated on three years ago when her right breast was removed; this she thinks is the cause. Her doctor wants her to go to Blackburn infirmary again, "but having five children dont feel inclined to".

Distrust of the usual professional advice is not uncommon. A London woman who has had seven children and one still-birth, is 42 years old, and not in bad circumstances. She cannot however afford any help, and says she has no time to rest with such a large family. She had severe post-natal trouble after the two last children (aged 4 and 3) and has "never been herself since." She also suffers from rheumatism and "aching legs". But she adds "Dont believe in doctors, had too many of them."

A woman in Rotherham, the wife of a miner, who has five children and has had two miscarriages, is 43. She has had very bad headaches and went to the doctor who advised having her eyes tested. "Did so, but was found to have perfect sight;" this evidently made her sceptical because she has consulted no-one for her rheumatism as she is "sure they can't help". She also had severe pains in the lower part of her back, which was so bad that she did go to her doctor, who told her that "all women got backache round about 40, so why worry. (I don't)". This woman is a midwife; one of her sons is a complete invalid and she has to do everything for him, lifting him, dressing him, making his bed (which takes two hours). She has an excellent diet, (the invalid son has special food which has to be cooked separately) and spends her "leisure" in writing up her midwifery records !

"So why worry?" They don't ! It is all summed up in that phrase. Only the strongest of these women *can* possibly be well; the hard work and entirely inadequate funds make it impossible for them to lead healthy lives. Most of them make the start hoping that things will by the grace of God turn out better for themselves than for their mothers, if they have been aware of the intensity of the struggle of their parents and of the weariness and premature old age that it has meant for the mothers. But in all probability the excitement of courtship, and marriage, the pride in the first home of her own, however humble, and the joyful anticipation and arrival of the first child, even of the second one perhaps, buoy up the spirit of the young woman and persuade her that all will be well with her. This has been expressed many times by the women who have been visited in this investigation, especially by those who have had the courage to face the collapse of their hopes with conscious realization of the disillusionment. There is then no alternative but to accept it, and to make the best of it. The husband and children must come first and as more than her energy and strength are consumed in this first care, she is obliged to omit the extra effort needed for herself. It is, of course a vicious circle; if she could be better she would make a better job of her work for the family; but circumstances are all against her and the outside agencies which seek to help her only, so far, touch the fringe of her problem. About this she can do nothing for she certainly has no time to think about or help to change the social organization in which she lives. So, indeed, why worry?

CHAPTER V

THE DAY'S WORK

"I BELIEVE myself that one of the biggest difficulties our mothers have is our husbands do not realise we ever need any leisure time. My life for many years consisted of being penned in a kitchen 9 feet square, every fourteen months a baby, as I had five babies in five years at first, until what with the struggle to live and no leisure I used to feel I was just a machine, until I had my first breakdown, and as dark as it was and as hard as it was it gave me the freedom and privilege of having an hour's fresh air. And so I truly know this is the lot of many a poor mother. I know my third baby had rickets, but what could I do, I was expecting another little one and already had a baby three years of age and one two years. So many of our men think we should not go out until the children are grown up. We do not want to be neglecting the home but we do feel we like to have a little look around the shops, or if we go to the Clinic we can just have a few minutes. . . . It isn't the men are unkind. It is the old idea we should always be at home."

Not many of the women go into such detail as this about the trials of their lives, but the record given of hours spent at work, the size of the family, the inability to pay for any help outside, the inconvenience of the house, the lack of adequate utensils and of decent clothes—let alone any small household or personal luxury—yields a picture in which monotony, loneliness, discouragement and sordid hard work are the main features,—a picture of almost unredeemed drabness. It is not that all of the women are unhappy as the writer of the above letter manifestly is. Taken as a whole, their vitality must be prodigious, for, in spite of every possible embarrassment, life goes on undiminished in bulk, even if with a lessening vigour and enjoyment. Happiness, like health, can suffer an almost unperceived lowering of standard, which results in a pathetic gratitude for what might be called negative mercies, the respite for an hour a day, for instance, from the laboriousness of the other eleven, twelve or thirteen; the help that a kind husband will "occasionally give on washing days, when he comes home from work," the relief when a major disaster which threatened one of the children (in the case of a woman in Leeds whose eldest son lost one eye in an accident and was threatened with the loss of the other) was "miraculously overcome".

It is little comfort that these women have learnt to accept their lot with so little complaint, often with such cheeriness and apparent satisfaction. For they are the mothers of the new generation and their outlook must to a certain extent be passed on to their daughters who will harbour no more than a vague hope that somehow, and through no direct action of their own, matters will have improved by the time they embark on the business of wife and mother. But that they do not raise the banner outside their own homes is neither surprising nor discreditable. Throughout their lives they have been faced with the tradition that the crown of a woman's life is to be a wife and mother. Their primary ambition is therefore satisfied. Everyone is pleased when they get married, most of all the great public, who see therein the working of Nature's divine and immutable laws. If for the woman herself the crown turns out to be one of thorns, that again must be Nature's inexorable way. It would be presumptuous on her part to think that she could or should do anything to change it. It is little short of a miracle that some women, even some of the most hard-worked, find time and mental energy to belong to such organisations as the Women's Co-operative Guild, the Salvation Army or a branch of their political party where they can hear and talk about the wider aspects of their own or other people's problems. It is, however, very rare to find amongst the active members of these organisations, the women whose poverty and consequent hard work demand the greatest measure of consideration and carefully planned reform. The poorest women *have no time* to spare for such immedi- ately irrelevant considerations as the establishment of a different system, a better education, a more comprehensive medical service, or some sort of organised co-operation. They are not themselves going to be given the second chance, whatever reforms may be introduced, and mean- time they have their twelve or thirteen or fourteen hours' work to do every day and their own day to day life to lead. It cannot stop, it cannot be interrupted; no-one else can do any of their jobs; and even if there is anyone else, like an adolescent daughter or a kind husband, this would mean losing time at any rate for a little while the pupil was learning; it might mean one meal at least being spoilt, one saucepan allowed to boil over, and there is no margin whatever for such waste, such loss of time; it requires less thought, even less physical energy to do the job oneself.

This is not a question of health. Whatever the condi- tion of fitness, the mother who does the work for a whole family of husband and three or more children has a titanic job under present conditions. If she is fortunate enough to be abnormally strong, she will manage to keep up with it, as long as her daily routine is not checked by some unusual misfortune. But if the ordinary round is harder than her body is strong her health must surely suffer with the result that she will find the course more and more difficult to hold; the less able she is to get through her task, the harder it will become . . . a circle of peculiar and tragic viciousness.

For the majority of the 1,250 women under review the ordinary routine seems to be as follows. Most of them get up at 6.30. If their husband and/or sons are miners, or bakers, or on any nightshift, they may have to get up at 4 (possibly earlier), make breakfast for those members of the family, and then, if they feel disposed to further sleep, go back to bed for another hour's rest. The same woman who does this has probably got a young child or even a baby, who wakes up early, and sleeping in the same room will in no case give his mother much peace after 6 a.m. If there is a suckling baby as well, (and it must be remembered that the woman who has had seven or eight children before the age of 35 has never been without a tiny baby or very young child,) she will have had to nurse him at least as late as 10 the night before. There are many complaints of children who for some reason or other disturb the night's rest. Her bed is shared not only by her husband but, in all probability, by one *at least* of her young family. Sleeplessness is not often spoken of in this investigation, because it is not considered an ailment, but it is quite clear that a good night's rest in a well-aired, quiet room and in a comfortable, well-covered bed, is practically unknown to the majority of these mothers. A woman can become accustomed to very little sleep just as she can to very little food.

When once she is up there is no rest at all till after dinner. She is on her legs the whole time. She has to get her husband off to work, the children washed, dressed and fed and sent to school. If she has a large family, even if she has only the average family of this whole group, four or five children, she is probably very poor and therefore lives in a very bad house, or a house extremely inadequately fitted for her needs. Her washing up will not only therefore be heavy, but it may have to be done under the worst conditions. She may have to go down (or up) two or three flights of stairs to get her water, and again to empty it away. She may have to heat it on the open fire, and she may have to be looking after the baby and the toddler at the same time. When this is done, she must clean the house. If she has the average family, the rooms are very "full of beds", and this will make her cleaning much more difficult than if she had twice the number of rooms with half the amount of furniture in each. She lacks the utensils too; and lacking any means to get hot water except by the kettle on the fire, she will be as careful as possible not to waste a drop. The school-children will be back for their dinner soon after 12, so she must begin her cooking in good time. Great difficulties confront her here. She has not got more than one or two saucepans and a frying pan, and so even if she is fortunate in having some proper sort of cooking stove, it is impossible to cook a dinner as it should be cooked, slowly and with the vegetables separately; hence the ubiquitous stew, with or without the remains of the Sunday meat according to the day of the week. She has nowhere to store food, or if there is cupboard room, it is inevitably in the only living room and probably next to the fireplace. Conditions may be so bad in this respect that she must go out in the middle of her morning's work to buy for dinner. This has the advantage of giving her and the baby a breath of fresh air during the morning; otherwise, unless there is a garden or yard, the baby, like herself is penned up in the 9 ft. square kitchen during the whole morning.

Dinner may last from 12 till 3. Her husband or a child at work may have quite different hours from the school-children, and it is quite usual to hear this comment. Very often she does not sit down herself to meals. The serving of five or six other people demands so much jumping up and down that she finds it easier to take her meals standing. If she is nursing a baby, she will sit down for that, and in this way "gets more rest". She does this after the children have returned to school. Sometimes the heat and stuffiness of the kitchen in which she has spent all or most of her morning takes her off her food, and she does not feel inclined to eat at all, or only a bite when the others have all finished and gone away. Then comes the same process of washing up, only a little more difficult because dinner is a greasier meal than breakfast. After that, with

luck at 2 or 2.30 but sometimes much later, if dinner for
any reason has had to go on longer, she can tidy herself
up and REST, or GO OUT, or SIT DOWN.

Leisure is a comparative term. Anything which is
slightly less arduous or gives a change of scene or occupation
from the active hard work of the eight hours for which
she has already been up is leisure. Sometimes, perhaps
once a week, perhaps only once a month, the change will
be a real one. She may go to the Welfare Centre with
baby, or to the recreation ground with the two small
children, or to see her sister or friend in the next street,
but most times the children don't give her the opportunity
for this sort of leisure, for there is sewing and mending and
knitting to be done for them; and besides there is always
the shopping to be done, and if she possibly can, she
does like to rest her legs a bit and sit down. So unless
there is some necessity to go out, she would rather on
most days stay indoors. And she may not have any clothes
to go out in, in which case the school children will do the
shopping after school hours. (Clothes are a great difficulty,
"practically an impossibility".)

Then comes tea, first the children's and then her
husband's, when he comes home from work; and by the
time that is all over and washed up it is time the children
began to go to bed. If she is a good manager she will
get them all into bed by 8, perhaps even earlier, and then
at last, at last, "a little peace and quietude !" She sits
down again, after having been twelve or fourteen hours
at work, mostly on her feet, (and this means *standing*
about, not *walking*,) and perhaps she then has a "quiet
talk with hubby", or listens to the wireless, "our one
luxury". Perhaps her husband reads the paper to her
She has got a lot of sewing to do, so she doesn't read much
to herself, and she doesn't go out because she can't leave
the children unless her husband undertakes to keep house
for one evening a week, while she goes to the pictures or
for a walk. There is no money to spare anyhow for the

pictures, or very seldom. She may or may not have a bite of supper with her husband, cocoa and bread and butter, or possibly a bit of fried fish. And so to her share of the bed, mostly at about 10.30 or 11.

This is the way that she spends six days out of seven, Sundays included, although Sunday may bring a slightly different arrangement of her problems because the shops are shut, the children and husband are at home. If she has been able to train her family well, and has got a good husband, they will relieve her of a little of the Sunday work, but it must be remembered that the husband is the breadwinner and must have his rest—and the children are young and will have their play. With luck, however, the mother will get "a nice quiet read on Sundays"— or a pleasant walk, or a visit to or from a friend; sometimes, if she is disposed that way, a quiet hour in church or chapel. But for her the seventh day is washing day, the day of extra labour, of extra discomfort and strain. At all times and in all circumstances it is arduous, but if she is living in the conditions in which thousands of mothers live, having to fetch water from the bottom floor of a four-storied house or from 100-200 yards or even a quarter of a mile along the village street; if she has nowhere to dry the clothes (and these include such bed-clothes as there may be) except in the kitchen in which she is cooking and the family is eating, the added tension together with the extra physical exertion, the discomfort of the house as well as the aching back, make it the really dark day of the week. There is no avoidance of it. Even if she could raise the money to send the washing out— she hasn't got the second set of clothes or bed coverings which this necessitates. The bed clothes have to be used again, possibly on the same day as washing.

There is also no avoidance of the other great labour which is superimposed on the ordinary round, the labour of child-bearing. The work will have to be done in the same way for those nine months before the baby comes and for the two or three months after she is about again but still not feeling "quite herself". The baby will probably be born in the bed which has already been described, the bed shared by other members of the family, and in the room of the use of which, even if she can get the bed to herself for a week, she cannot possibly deprive the family for more than a few hours. It is out of the question, she thinks, to go to hospital, and to leave her husband and children either to fend for themselves—or to the care of a stranger, or of an already overworked but friendly neighbour. Even if she is in bed, she is at least in her own home; and can direct operations, even perhaps doing some of the "smaller" jobs herself—like drying crockery, ironing[1], and of course the eternal mending. How is it possible that she should stay in bed for long enough to regain her full physical strength, the strength that has been taxed not only in the actual labour of child-birth, but in six or seven of the preceding months, when every household duty has been more difficult to accomplish and has involved a far greater strain than it does when she is in her "normal" health? If she is sensible, she will have got help from the Clinic, extra milk if she is very poor, and tonics and, perhaps, if she is fortunate enough to live in an enlightened municipality, a good meal once a day for herself. But her scene and her work will not have changed, and unless she goes into hospital for the confinement, it cannot bring that rest and comfort which she needs and deserves, but only extra difficulties for everyone in the family and very often serious ill-health for herself.

So the days, the weeks, the months, the years go on. There may be a break for an hour or two in the month when she attends some Guild or Women's Institute meeting. Once a year there may be a day's outing; but a holiday

[1] The writer found one woman sitting up in bed three days after the birth of her sixth baby ironing on a tray across her knees; the iron was handed to her by a neighbour who was washing up the dinner.

in the sense of going away from home, eating food she has
not herself cooked, sleeping in another bed, living in a
different scene, meeting other people and doing the things
she can never do at home,—this has been unheard of
since the family arrived. She cannot go without the family,
and there can be no question of taking them too. Possibly
the children are somehow or other got into the country
for a few days in the summer, if they live in the town;
but it is without mother, unless she will go hop-picking,
taking the small children with her. But it is only a very,
very few who get the chance of even this "holiday". There
is—again for the very few—another possibility of a holiday
—convalescence. If the mother has been "really ill" she
may be sent away by the hospital or under some insurance
scheme, or by the Salvation Army or by one of the agencies
whose merciful function it is to procure this kind of inter-
mission for the woman whose strength has at last given
way. She is sent away . . . away from her home, away
from the smell of inferior and inadequately prepared
food, away from the noise and worry of her family, away
to the sea, for a fortnight or even three weeks. It may
be that she is too ill to get much active enjoyment out of
it, but oh, the blessedness of the rest, the good food, the
comfortable bed, the difference of scene for her eyes, the
glorious feeling of having nothing to do. "As dark as it
was and as hard as it was, it gave me the privilege of
having an hour's fresh air."

But if illness has been so severe as to merit this magnificent
atonement, it has meant months probably of crippling
indisposition which has added enormously to the burden
of work, and robbed it of all that potential satisfaction
that can be found in the fulfilment of her task. She has
had to let things slide, and she has slipped back so far
that it will take months and months to catch up again even
to her old standard of order and efficiency. This, in her
eyes, is probably the worst disaster than can happen—
her own illness. Other disasters are bound to come in the

ordinary course of family life; the sickness of a child—the unemployment of her husband—the care of an old and perhaps tiresome grandparent. But if she can keep fit, she will meet the extra burden. She may even voluntarily adopt another child, whose parents are dead; or she will augment the family income by going out to work herself, somehow or other squeezing her own house-work into shorter hours. It may be a little less efficient, but the compensation is that she has a little more money for food, and can get better cooking utensils. At whatever cost of labour and effort a little more money is what she really wants; that is the magic which unties the Gordian knot. But there is little opportunity for this, and the poorer she is, the more difficult it is to arrange things in her own home so as to make it possible to leave it for even a couple of hours a day. Where it *must* be done, as in the case of a widow, or a woman with an invalid husband, the strain is nearly always almost insupportable.

Naturally there are some who seem to get more out of life than others; but almost without exception it is those women who have very few children, one, two or at the most three, and who for this or some other reason are in much better financial circumstances, who are able to get more real rest and change of scene and to employ their leisure in some way which suggests an interest in outside things. But there are not more than half a dozen who speak of politics, literary interests, study of any sort or music. The cinema is very rarely mentioned, and many women say that they have *never* been to the pictures. A few who live in the country speak of walking and gardening; others of going to chapel or church on Sundays. An overwhelming proportion say that they spend their "leisure" in sewing and doing other household jobs, slightly different from the ordinary work of cooking and house-cleaning.

The subject of husbands could form a thesis by itself. They are not very often specifically mentioned in the answers to this interrogatory, except in regard to their occupation and the money with which they provide their wives for housekeeping. But when a man adds to the embarrassments of life by bad temper or drunkenness, or is exasperatingly impatient with the wife's ill-health or unsympathetic with her difficulties, he generally appears in the list of her grievances directly or by implication. It is more often the visitor than the wife who makes special note of him. Equally, great solicitude for or sympathy with his wife is specially commended in a husband. Many instances are given of the husband carrying heavy tubs or coals for his wife—keeping watch over the children one evening a week, so that she can go out—reading aloud to her— or—if she is really ill—looking after her with great care, as far as his occupation allows. But the impression given in general of the attitude of the husbands in this enquiry is that of the quotation at the head of this chapter:— "our husbands do not realize we ever need any leisure". With the best will in the world, it is difficult for a man to visualize his wife's day—the loneliness, the embarrassments of her work, the struggle to spend every penny of his money to the best advantage. In most cases he can count upon her devoted service to himself and to their children,— and he feels instinctively that her affection gives a pleasant flavour to her work which is absent from his own—and that she is fortunate in not being under the orders of an employer, and subject to regulations of time and speed of work etc. etc. If he is unemployed and therefore spends more time at home, the additional worry for both of them will take precedence of all other difficulties, and if he then notices the harassing conditions of her life, he will attribute them largely to this cause. Besides, the unemployed man can and does generally give his wife some help in the housework, which does much to lighten her physical burden, although it is little compensation for the additional mental worry.

Note is sometimes made in the women's accounts of the help given to them by the older of their schoolchildren.

It is very usual to find mention of a child being kept back from school to do some of the work that the mother is too ill to do. Only a few mothers speak of training their children to help in the house as part of a regular routine—but this is probably less rare than it appears to be. It must be realized, however, that any help that a child under twelve can give costs so much in supervision and probably worry for a careful mother, that she feels it is easier to send the child out of the way and get on with the job herself. This may be a short-sighted policy, but it is easily forgiven in the woman who has no time to organize or plan.

It may be said that, even granting that there is no exaggeration in the above account of the working-class mother's life, there is no ground for giving special consideration to her case as apart from that of the father and the children; that their lot is just as hard as hers, and that the want from which she suffers is equally severe for them. That in many respects this is so, cannot be denied; but it is abundantly clear from the accounts given by the women themselves in this investigation that they are subject to many hardships from which circumstance or they themselves protect their families. To begin with, the working mother is almost entirely cut off from contact with the world outside her house. She eats, sleeps, "rests", on the scene of her labour, and her labour is entirely solitary. However arduous or unpleasant the man's work has been, the hours of it are limited and he then leaves not only the work itself but the place of it behind him for fourteen or sixteen hours out of every twenty-four. Even if he cannot *rest* in this time, he changes his occupation and his surroundings. If he is blessed with a capable hard-working wife, his home will represent to him a place of ease and quiet after an eight or ten hour day spent in hard, perhaps dangerous toil. He will have had ample opportunity for talking with his fellows, of hearing about the greater world, of widening his horizon. The children have equally either been out at work or at school, where for many hours of the day they have lived in airy well-lighted rooms, with ample space for movement and for play. They too have met and talked with their fellows, and whatever the deprivations of their home, they go there to find that someone else has prepared their food, mended their clothes, and generally put things in order. Naturally they suffer, as the father does too, from the poverty of the home, the lack of sufficient food and clothes and warmth and comfort, but it is undoubtedly true that even in these respects the mother will be the first to go without. Her husband *must* be fed, as upon him depends the first of all necessities, money. The children must or will be fed, and the school will if necessary supplement. Equally husband and children must be clothed, not only fairly warmly but for school or work fairly decently. She need not be; she need not even go out, so it is not *absolutely* necessary for her to have an outdoor coat. And lastly, whatever the emotional compensations, whatever her devotion, her family creates her labour, and tightens the bonds that tie her to the lonely and narrow sphere of "home". The happiness that she often finds in her relationship of wife and mother is as miraculous as it is compensatory.

Much might be done even without dealing with the basic evil of poverty and without disintegrating the sacred edifice of the home, to introduce some ease into the lives of these women and so to lighten their work that they would have time to rest, to make contacts with the outer world, and to enjoy some at least of those cultural and recreative pursuits which would release them spiritually as well as physically from their present slavery. First of all, domestic and household training. As the Essex woman, quoted at the head of the preceding chapter, writes further on in her description of her life "Never having been trained to housework, I find it very difficult to run my home efficiently—very small allowance prevents purchase of many labour-saving devices." If this is said of housework, how much oftener can it be said of more skilled work such as cooking and household management. Very few of these women know how to make *the best* of their slender resources by the wise expenditure either of money or of time. Better housing with equipment designed *to the very special needs of the woman who does all her own work* and every opportunity, if not compulsion to learn her trade would immediately release her from much of her present bondage. As to the lack of labour-saving devices, she might with gentle persuasion be induced to make use of certain communal amenities where these are too expensive to instal in her individual house. Communal wash-houses, bakehouses, sewing rooms with good machines, should all be within easy reach of her home, for her use for a minute charge which would be less than she spends in individual firing at home; they would mean an immense saving of time and therefore indirectly of money expended in the attempt to do an expert job without the proper tools. This would also serve the very desirable purpose of bringing her in the course of her daily work into contact with other women doing the same job, and she would no longer have to find out for herself the better ways of doing things. And she should have also not too far from her home a club to which at any time in the week she can go to seek rest and companionship, cultural and recreative occupation and a blessed change of scene. If her work has been eased in the ways suggested above, she will find time for this, just as somehow now, she sometimes finds time for the weekly visit to the Welfare Centre with her babies. Here she could read, educate herself, talk to other women, listen, if she wanted to, to lectures, and get advice and help on any problem that worried her. Here too she should be able to bring her husband or friends for games or "socials"; but it should be *her* club, designed above all to meet *her* needs and to bring her enjoyment in whatever form she sought it. And lastly she should have a holiday "with pay" once a year. She should be able for a week or a fortnight completely to stop work. Someone else must cook and clean and mend and bend not only for her husband and children but for herself. There is absolutely nothing revolutionary in any of these suggestions. It is as clear as day that even in the difficult question of finance they will save so much in sickness, hospital expenses and all the bolstering activities for which at present the nation is so heavily taxed, that they would very soon become self-supporting and be entirely free from that flavour of charity which is rightly so distasteful to the millions whose first wish is to be independent and to be enabled of themselves to lead the lives of human beings.

Facts gathered from the forms in support of the foregoing description

About half the women get up at 6.30 or a little before and go to bed at 10.30 or 11. In the country these hours tend to be a little earlier at both ends. Half the women say they are twelve hours or more a day on their feet. Of the other half a very few are a great deal less than this, but only if they are old and their children grown up, or if they have very few children, or if they are severely crippled by some illness. The majority (about 65%) say they have two hours' "leisure" in the day,—but this is spent in shopping, taking the baby out, mending, sewing and doing household jobs of an irregular kind which cannot be fitted into "working hours", such as tidying cupboards, repapering a room, gardening etc.

Some women get up at 3 or 4 and never have a period of more than four hours at a time of unbroken sleep. If they have two men working on different shifts, e.g. miners, tram-conductors, bakers etc., the housework is very much more difficult, owing to having to arrange for quiet sleep during the day for one or more members of the family.

Leisure

It seems nearly always true that even when a woman has reached middle age and has not so much to do, she has very few intelligent interests unless she has either been better educated than most, or has had a small family and therefore more time when she was young to cultivate some hobby or to follow an intellectual study. In some pathetic cases the older woman who has had a large family who are now grown up is actively unhappy and finds time extremely heavy on her hands.

Mrs. N. of Bolton is 52, and has two children. She was an elementary school teacher before marriage; her husband is a clerk-of-works, and she has £4 housekeeping money. She does not get any "real leisure in the afternoons, or very seldom, but every evening. Usually visit friends, sew, attend lectures, women's meetings, study crosswords, attend concerts and an occasional good film." Her only complaint is "dreadful monotony".

An elderly woman in Cardiff is very poor and has had eight children, of whom only two are now of school age. She says she hasn't any difficulties about her work "*now*— I feel fairly well—but I have had a hard time when the children were young. I usually sit down quietly in the evenings sewing or thinking. I do very little reading and I very seldom go out in the evening or attend any meetings or other socials. It gets a little dreary".

When there are a lot of young children it is miraculous when any real leisure is procurable. Many women say they cannot leave the children in the evening; a woman in Blackburn says "Never go to Market or Cinema. Sister used to come and look after children and let me go out, but has now removed from the town". She is 35, has had six children of whom the first one died, and is in extremely bad health. She has had varicose veins for the last six years, for which the doctor has advised elastic stockings and arch supports, but she cannot afford them. She is very anæmic, and two years ago "the Doctor told me it was anæmia and gave me some medicine, but I know it is not enough food. Also when I have had influenza twice since Christmas, he told me I must go to bed but it is impossible when you have all these children". Her house is very old, damp and dark, but she says she never goes out. The visitor writes, "This mother has never tasted herrings. I suggested them and she asked how to cook them and did I think they would be the things her mother used to cook on a fork in front of the fire ! She is a very good mother but in terribly poor health." A woman in Leeds manages to get one hour once a week at "Mother's meeting at the Chapel. I dont count the other times that I sit down to mend or knit for the kiddies" (seven of them). Another Leeds woman says "never get out except to shop; have never been to the talkies". Mrs. T. of Derby, whose housing conditions are described on page 144 "sits down for feeding the baby, but takes her own meals standing. She is in very poor health, having had bad kidney trouble with the first and third babies. . . . Her surroundings are squalid, and there is no water or sink in the house. . . . She has never been to a talkie". (Extract from visitor's report.)

A woman in Caerphilly has five children, the eldest 13. Her health is good except for teeth. She says she is on her feet for 16½ hours a day, sometimes more, and about leisure she writes—"After my children go to bed, i gets two hours rest, if call it rest, i am mending my children's clothes and tidying in those few hours i get". But a woman in a country town in Essex, with seven children all under 13, and in a good Council house, makes a point of going once a week to the pictures with her husband, "for a rest and a little pleasure".

A woman in Stafford has a Council house in which there are no drawbacks. She has two children and is in good health. She works all day, but gives her evenings to "rest and quiet enjoyment. I read a lot, like walking and going

to chapel". Mrs. P. of Accrington is 30; her husband is a
book-binder and gives her £3 a week. She has only one
child; she goes to League of Nations meetings, night-
classes and lectures, occasional concerts. A woman in
Edinburgh has a great interest in politics; she too has an
only child, now grown up. Both of these women are in
comfortable financial circumstances and are in good
health.

Mrs. S. lives in the country. She is 45, and she has had
four children of whom only the youngest, a girl of 14, is
living at home. Her husband is a gardener, and she has a
good cottage. Her leisure time is in the afternoons and
evenings. She knits, reads, sews, shops, walks and goes to
whist drives. She is not at all healthy. She has goitre, for
which her doctor has given her iodized salt, but she cannot
afford regular attendance from him which she thinks she
ought to have. She has ulcerated legs owing to her hard
work when she was pregnant and when the children were
younger. She has been under ten doctors for this, and two
hospitals ! She has bad dermatitis, caused by a lead lotion
which one doctor gave her for her leg and which poisoned
the whole system. She says about this:—"Its no good
going to doctors about things which there's only one
cure for—less work and more rest". Her special difficulties
now are "Washing is the worst as it is apt to make my hands
bad, and the standing is bad for my leg".

It is fairly easy to detect those country villages, where
there is a good deal of organised recreation, such as a
well-run Women's Institute—Church Socials and outside
lectures. Several women in Essex live in such villages; for
instance—Mrs. T. is the wife of a farm labourer in Essex.
She is 31 and has two children only. She is perfectly strong.
"Women's Institute meetings, (once a month) and Choir
practices (once a week) afford really the leisure hours, and
evenings spent mending and making clothes."

A woman in another Essex village speaks of "work for
the Institute; singing practise,—dancing once a week".

She, too, has only two children. And a widow in Essex who has four children, an "old-fashioned difficult cottage" and goes out to work in the village every day for 6d. an hour—finds time for "choir practise, political meetings, Women's Institute and dancing".

Very occasionally games are mentioned, played with the children or husband. A woman in Sheffield who is very poor, lives in a slum house, and has four children, is in extremely bad health. She says she must rest sometimes during the day—and she sometimes plays cards or ludo "as that is cheaper than the pictures—I have no money for pictures." Another woman mentions jig-saw puzzles—and another crossword puzzles.

But even if their work has never been very hard, they often seem unable to take any interest in life except the immediate care of the home, on which they will, in these circumstances, spend many unnecessary hours. Mrs. B. of Heston is 43 and has no children. She has very good health except for a little rheumatism. She gets plenty of leisure which she spends "about the house; I have no hobbies; I read the paper or listen to the wireless and very occasionally go for a walk or visit a neighbour". And Mrs. Y. of Bolton is 38, has no children and is very well. She gets five hours' leisure in the day, and sews or visits. "I never read, not even the paper."

Others, however, mention "healthful and uplifting interests" if their work is not too hard. Mrs. F. of Rotherham is 31 and has only two children. Her husband is a motor lorry-driver and she is fairly well off. She is not in very good health, and is very communicative about her symptoms, which she seems rather to enjoy. She writes "I am interested in any health topic. At school we had lesons (sic) in health and hygiene. I am invited to a Keep fit Class in connection with the social side of the Church. I am a member of a concert party and was for many years a member of a choral society. All these things I believe to be uplifting and healthful. My husband and I work in co-operation with all things and share the family responsibilities. I am a member of the Fellowship of marriage (St. John's branch). Evenings are set aside for healthful discussions which broaden the outlook and improve the mind."

It makes an incredible difference to the amount of leisure that a mother gets, if she is an efficient manager. Even with great practical difficulties in her work, she will organize things so that she can follow her outside interests. Naturally a convenient house and a little less anxiety about money contribute to make this possible. Here is a good example of a very hard-working woman who nevertheless takes obvious pleasure in the interests she has outside her home. She lives in a South-Eastern suburb of London in a Council house, which has four rooms and for which she pays 18/9 rent out of total housekeeping money of £3 10s. 0d. She is 38 and has four children (and has had one miscarriage). Her children range from seventeen years to thirteen months. She writes about her house "Nothing to grumble about, only should like one a little larger—say one other room. My husband works on shift work at the Flour Mills. When he is on night work its very difficult to try and keep quiet, also not being able to go upstairs to clean as often as I like, also when he works afternoons. I do practically all my work then." She suffers a little from her eyes and had an operation after a miscarriage six years ago. She makes regular payments to the Hospital Savings Association and to the Nursing Association. She gets up at 6.30 and goes to bed at 11 or 12 "according to husband's work". But nevertheless on "Monday afternoons I go to Women's meeting 3 to 4.30, Wed: afternoon to sewing meeting in connection with Bazaar at local church, Thursday afternoon go to Children's welfare with baby for instructions about Baby". Further she writes: "I should like to add that 5 years ago I had two serious operations at Cottage hospital and I was there for four months. I was very weak when I came out and I went to Bexhill-on-Sea for three weeks under the H.S.A.[1] scheme. It was the most lovely holiday. Since the birth of last child I have felt wonderfully well. Also in my spare moments I make childrens clothes including all babies' which saves a great deal of money. Apart from this, I take a keen interest in gardening and keeping garden in order."

A woman in Eltham (near Woolwich) is 35 and has six children, all under 14. She is in a Council house of four rooms, for which she pays 14/7—and it has "no internal difficulties but merely lies low and has railway at back". She is in good health and has 38/- housekeeping money after the payment of rent. Her husband is employed in Woolwich Arsenal. She gets two hours "*regular*" leisure a day, and knits and reads or mends, and plays the piano. She worked as a ward-maid in a hospital for four years before her marriage. Her only difficulty is "managing the money".

Such cases however are the exception. It is much more usual to read that in effect such leisure time as there is is spent in some sedentary occupation as a rest from the long hours of standing—and that it is spent entirely in mending. Mrs. E. of Forest Gate, East London, is 38 and has six children. She says firmly that she gets no leisure till the evening when the children are in bed and then "I just sit still and say, at last a bit of peace and quietness".

The woman whose hard work and poverty have crushed her, probably finds time to hang about a good deal in spite of a large family and an inconvenient house. Here is an unhappy woman outside Durham who, according to the Health Visitor "has had such a hard struggle under very unfortunate circumstances that one doesn't know now how to help her. The main worry here is small income. Rent is 7/- (out of £1 17s. 0d. housekeeping) 4/- paid weekly to clothing club; 2/- for boots and bedding, 6d. spent on cigarettes. . . . Her husband is very dogmatic

[1] Hospitals Saving Association.

and treats her unkindly. He very often demands a cooked supper at mid-night. The mother is very quiet (which means a strain) for a peaceable life. She takes advice about the children but never thinks about herself". This family of parents and six children under 13 live in a three-roomed tenement flat, in a very noisy street. "Busses pass from Newcastle to outlying districts from 5.30 a.m. to midnight. Have no wash-house, and coal-house is downstairs; clothes are boiled on kitchen fire, stairs are very tiring". The mother is 37 and has had eight children of whom two have died of pneumonia. She gets up at 7 and goes to bed "midnight or 12.30", and is on her feet all the time. She feels very ill but says that except for headaches, constipation and toothache she doesn't know what is the matter. In answer to the question about leisure, she says, "I don't know what I do,—I stay about the house, sometimes, but not often take children for a walk, but I haven't any outdoor clothes, so I chat to neighbours two or three times daily and sit on back step mending and darning". The visitor says "This woman has never been to a Picture House; she does all the washing and bread-baking at home".

A Birmingham bus driver's wife makes the most succinct and cogent of all records of leisure. She has five children, all under 9, a poor house and is on her feet all day. Her health is fairly good but she is very poor. About leisure she says "sit on step if fine and read if wet". (The two occupations appear to be incompatible !)

Husbands

Mrs. D. of Glasgow is 36. She has ten children, all living at home, and all under 15. In addition she has had one miscarriage. For three years she has suffered from spinal trouble, the cause of which has not been medically diagnosed, but Mrs. D. says it "caused probably by worry about the children, and about husband's unemployment".

She is taking phospherine and the doctor wants her "to go to hospital for a womb operation" as she had post-natal trouble after the still-birth ten years ago (since when she has had six children). She finds her work very hard as she has to sit down very often,—and her eldest daughters (twins of 15) are able to help her a certain amount,—but they go out to work. They get the breakfast, so that she need not get up till ten-o'clock. Mrs. D. does not drink water as it gives her a pain, but she drinks a lot of tea. Her diet is fair. She lives in a Council flat of four rooms, for which she pays 9/6 rent out of £2 4s. 0d. total income. The Health Visitor writes "Mrs. D. is very much crippled with her trouble, and according to the doctor it is due to constant worry. Each new arrival was a cause for fresh anxiety. Husband also causes worry owing to gambling habits, or inattention to home. He lost good employment through his inattention to business (and has now been unemployed for several years). Mrs. D. is considered incurable. She refuses to go into hospital as she worries about the children at home. She is an excellent mother".

Mrs. W. of Durham is 39. She has had nine children and one still-birth. Two premature babies died at the age of a few weeks, and one of pneumonia at 18 months old. Five of the children live at home. The family of seven live in a well-kept tenement flat. The husband is a post-man. Mrs. W. gets £3 1s. 0d. for housekeeping, including 15/– unemployment money from a son of 21. She pays 10/3 rent out of this. She is in very bad health, and in the last ten years has been twice curetted, has had radium treatment and now has had hysterectomy performed. She had pneumonia ten days after this operation. She suffers constantly from bad headaches, rheumatism, insomnia and constipation. She has never attended Child Welfare or Ante-natal Clinics, but calls in a private doctor when necessary. (She contributes 6d. a week to a "doctor's Club") She has an excellent diet. They have a small allotment in which they grow vegetables, and keep hens, and the postman fishes nearly every Sunday. Mrs. W. goes to Church every Sunday evening, to a Church Guild meeting once a week and to the Pictures once a week. All the washing, bread and cake baking are done at home. She does all the papering and painting of her rooms herself "with a little help from husband", but she adds "I wish I could afford assistance; husband keeps 15/- weekly pocket money and spends most of it in drink, very quiet man usually but quarrelsome in drink. This has just happened during the last four years, and is a bad example to the children". The Health Visitor writes, "This mother worries very much and has a difficult time, but is exceedingly plucky. She has a daughter of 16 with a tubercular kidney. This is another worry."

Mrs. S. of Caerphilly is 36 and has had eleven children, of whom two have died and two boys are away. She has £2 0s. 6d. for housekeeping and pays 8/- rent out of this for a good "working-class house in elevated position"— It has five rooms. She is a careful methodical woman; contributes to a doctor's club and has attended Ante-natal ("anti-natal"!) and Child Welfare clinics regularly. She says she is fairly well, but suffers from severe pain in back and side dating from the birth of the last child, four years ago. Her husband is unemployed and does all the washing for her, but "would rather he was working".

A woman in Rotherham lives in a Council house of four rooms, for which she pays 9/6 rent. It is damp and cold, the fireplace in the living-room is too small, and the bathroom is downstairs near the back door. She is 41, and has had thirteen pregnancies, including three still-births. Three children have died of tuberculosis. The seven living children are all at home. The mother herself is tubercular and attends the T.B. dispensary, and three of her children are on the T.B. register. She says she gets up "at 10 a.m. but should be up at half past seven, but husband out of work, he get up, as doctor say I must go easy". She says that her husband has been unemployed five years and she is "much worried with large family, three on T.B. register who go in sanatorium at times— been in three times myself, lak of housekeeping money to feed and cloth the children properly, son working likes pocket money cant give it to him large family make a lot of work three girls who could go out to work if they were well". She has attended the Birth Control Clinic, but obviously either too late or ineffectively.

Mrs. B. of Cardiff lives in a good house in a "residential" district, for which she pays 12/6 a week, out of housekeeping money of £2. Her husband is a coal-tipper in work. She was a "parlourmaid in good service" before marriage, and is a methodical, tidy-minded woman. She is 38 and has three young children. She suffers from "nerves ever since marriage owing to living with an aged inlaw who's method with children and other things was very different from my own". For this complaint Mrs. B. gets out "as much as Possible & Take an interest in making my childrens clothes and find knitting a great help". She has a fair diet and says "My housework is a Pleasure and Home Life would be more so, if only my Husband was a little more considerate in thinking how an hour away from it all and the children would make it so much easier and make Mother's outlook brighter. I might add I think the teaching of children to help in the House and shopping is a great help and saves Mother a lot, and can often rest her legs while they wash up dishes etc. which my girls of 7 and 10 years love to do and when Mother is not quite up to the mark it does not come a trail to them, and I can depend on them for most things without spoiling their Pleasures and I think when left, it such a boon to them to know how to shop and count change." Mrs. B.'s own mother was a trained nurse and taught her a great deal. She reads books on health, goes to the clinic "and when in Doubt asks Doctor's Advice".

Mrs. S. of East London is in extremely bad health. She is 31 and has had three children, of whom one has died, and four miscarriages. She is very anæmic, has bad teeth, bad back aches and severe discharge. Her husband is a baker, and "this makes the arrangement of the housework very difficult, as he wants to get to sleep before the children are in bed;—also he is rather exacting and has no sympathy with my state of health, unless I am actually confined to bed". Moreover, although he earns £3 10s. 0d. a week, he only allows her 32/6 for housekeeping, out of which she has to pay electric light, gas, coal, all food, and clothing for herself and the two children. She has a very poor diet, and says she does not enjoy her food. Owing to her bad health, she finds her work especially the washing extremely hard. She says she consults the doctor when there is a "definite illness, but then this has to be paid out of housekeeping, so it cannot happen often". Her leisure consists of a regular visit to a friend once a month, and a visit to the cinema once a week, ("not always regular").

Special Hardships

Of the special hardships which add tragedy to the already unendurable trials of the lives of these mothers, there is no lack. Mrs. W. of Paddington lives in a tenement "flat" of three rooms. She is 30 and has six children, three of whom are extremely delicate. She worries over them a lot and has to take them constantly to hospital for treatment. She has not the energy to look after herself "because looking after the children takes up all the time". She had pleural pneumonia herself a year ago since when her "chest has never been right, but it's this business of taking children to hospital in all weathers". Her housing difficulties too are very great. She has to fetch water from downstairs and empty it in the communal w.c. and for one week of the month she cleans the w.c. and all the stairs of the house. (Each tenant does this in turn). The visitor writes "This poor woman has an almost intolerable burden with her own poor health and sick children. Her husband's work necessitates her getting up at 5.30, and I have known her come to the hospital at 10 with the children, already so exhausted, that I have wanted to put her straight to bed".

Mrs. E. of Cardiff has seven children living at home. She is very poor, but pays 13/2 rent out of £1 12s. 0d. housekeeping money. She says that her health is fairly good, but she constantly feels dizzy, which she puts down to indigestion, which in turn is caused by having no teeth. She writes "At most times its hard to make things meet, and about eighteen months ago I lost a daughter after having her in bed for nine weeks. I had to do everything for her and I was continually up and down stairs and no sleep at night. That was a black time and of course her death upset me a lot, since then my husband have been in and out of work, so that I've had a lot of worry, those worries I think are the cause of me feeling depressed at times". But extra difficulties like this do not always crush or even depress the mother's spirit. Here is another woman in Cardiff who is 39 and has five children, the eldest of whom, a boy of 8, has only one leg, "which means that I have to do little jobs in the way of extra work. Table and bed-linen I send to the Laundry, the remainder I do myself. I do everything single-handed, and the only help I get for the babies is when a friend calls in occasionally on a fine afternoon to take them out. My domestic duties do not burden me much because on the whole I rather like it. In disposition I am bright and cheerful and as a result life in general does not appear too hard for me. I always plan my work on a weekly routine and endeavour to stick to the plan, provided the weather is not too exacting." Her husband is a shop-keeper, and she was a shop-assistant before marriage. She is very well; she always goes out with the babies in the afternoon, except when the friend calls in to take them, and in the evenings from 9 to 10.30 she reads and "talk with hubby".

Another cheerful woman is one who describes herself as the "Mother of Ten". She lives in Bethnal Green, and is 38. Two of the ten children have died, and she has had one still-birth. Her husband is unemployed. She is not very well; she has neuritis and gets very giddy because she did not have "enough to eat before birth of baby and no strength when time for baby's birth. Doctor said I was to do less housework and washing and get out more in the air. Nurse from Clinic said I was to take care of myself and have plenty of rest". She doesn't find her day's work too hard for her, but "tiring owing to amount of family. Leisure time is very scarce as children make work for all time; I take half an hour after dinner to rest and sew and read the paper in the evening. The only difficulties are unemployment and trying to make ends meet; housework does not worry me when I feel alright". As to teaching on health, she says she had "The same as children of today in schools cleanliness and go to bed early and get up early. She goes to bed at 11 and gets up at 6.30." They live in three rooms.

Mrs. P. of Brighton has had an extremely hard life. She is 46 and has had eight children and one miscarriage. Her husband is much older than herself and is unemployed and has the old-age pension. She adds, "He is ill-tempered, and no help at all in the house, which is a great trial of patience." Seven of her children still live at home and the youngest is 3. She pays 9/5 rent for an old house in a condemned area with only two bedrooms; (cf. another Brighton woman who has moved out of this kind of district to a Corporation house for which she pays 12/–; p. 130). Mrs. P. has 33/7 for food, clothes, cleaning utensils, etc., for herself and husband and all the children, except that two of the elder children buy their own clothes. She says in answer to the first question, Do you feel fit and well? "No, far from it." She has bronchitis every winter, bad phlebitis, bad headaches, rheumatism, and two years ago had a bad attack of pneumonia. She writes, "I feel that much of my ill-health is due to insufficient nourishment after child-birth and too short a time between confinements. I don't want to grumble, but I do wonder sometimes if things *are* going to get easier."

Mrs. K. of Durham gets up at 3 a.m. and then returns to bed after seeing her eldest son off to work. She gets up again at 7, and goes to bed at 11 p.m. She has had five children of whom one died. Her husband is an unemployed miner and she gets 38/– unemployment benefit, and 11/6, the boy's pay (he is 15). Her cottage for which she pays 7/9 rent is atrocious. One of the two bedrooms has only a skylight, the other a tiny window; the roof is bad and the rain comes in; the downstairs windows do not open (cf. another Durham woman quoted on p. 86). Her oven is defective; there is no gas, no bath, no electricity, and all pans have to be lifted on to an open fire. She is very anæmic, has "whiteleg", constipation and piles, bad dental caries ever since marriage, headaches, palpitation, faintness, and a year ago had paralysis in the right side of her face. Like many other Durham women, she is a wonderful housewife and mother. The children all have fresh milk for breakfast (she does not say how much), home-made bread, and eggs "frequently". She does her own papering and "possing". Her work is not made easier by the fact that her husband lost a leg in the War, and took to drink, "which caused much unhappiness and worry, but he seems to be better now." (She does not say whether she has cured him by her own efforts, but it seems likely.) She goes regularly to the doctor for all her ailments, but as his unvarying advice seems to be rest and less work, she cannot follow it.

Holidays

Cases have been quoted earlier (see pp. 51, 94, 113), in which the benefits and blessings of a holiday in a convalescent home have been acknowledged by the mothers. Here are others. A woman in Birmingham aged 40 has had eleven children, all living at home. She gets up at 5.30 and sees her husband, (an engineer) and elder children off to work, and then goes back to bed till 8. (She had a baby of three weeks old at the time she wrote her form.) For the last few years she has suffered from debility and has just returned from a fortnight's rest in a Convalescent home, "which teaches you the value of rest and regular meals; shouldn't have thought it could make so much difference".

Mrs. H. of Hampstead is 35 and has had five children, one miscarriage and one still-birth. She says "For fourteen years I been tied to the spot, as being caretakers some-one must always be here, no change or holidays through lack of money. Children need all we get, when depressed I think of others who are many times worse off and then I am thankful for all I have, 4 good children and a roof over our head. But I do think we mothers need some holiday sometimes." Mrs. H. is in very poor health and is a regular attendant at University College Hospital.

A mother in a small country town in Essex is 40 and had six children, all living at home and still at school. She suffers from psoriasis and kidney trouble. She pays 13/6 for part of an old cottage, out of £2 housekeeping money. There is no bathroom, and all water has to be heated on the fire. Her diet is very poor, she never eats meat, very seldom vegetables, (except potatoes and dried peas) and no supper. This does not follow out the doctor's advice of "rest and better food". She writes, "When I get my periods I get very depressed and tired, I cannot do much housework, it means too much to try and do afterwards, and since I had my last three children I do not gain enough energy to work as I would like. I really think mothers should have a holiday once a year, this is a great expense. I have had one spell of ten days in sixteen years."

Mrs. C. of Chesterfield is 55. She lives with her husband

who is an unemployed miner, and three sons aged 21,
19 and 12 in a very poor old cottage with no copper, no
bathroom, no coal-shed. She has to keep her coal in the
cellar where the food is kept, and to take out the food every
time she fetches coal. She has had eight children, of whom
two have died. The eldest son has always had a crippled
right arm, which "made it very difficult to maintain him;
now things are better as he has just come back from
cripples training college and started work with a good
firm. . . . I have been in hospital three times and once
went away to the sea afterwards, I remember that as long
as I live."

Unemployment

As has been seen before, unemployment is the worst
misfortune to bear bravely and only too often it comes on
top of other trials which have darkened the mother's
life. But it is not rare to find even in such circumstances
an unyielding maternal courage. Of Mrs. R. of Fulham
the visitor writes—"This woman never gives way. She
is determined that her standard shall not fall even through
periods of unemployment. Her house is very inconvenient
and badly overcrowded. But she feeds herself and her
family well and never complains". Mrs. R. is 49, has
had ten children of whom nine are living at home, and
three miscarriages. Her husband is a stoker in irregular
work. She lives in three rooms and there is a bathroom,
but no means of heating the water for it. She has had
varicose veins since 1920 due to childbearing aggravated
by continuous standing and working. She gets up at
5 a.m. *and does a newspaper round from* 5.30 *to* 6.30. She
says she is on her feet for 15–16 hours a day and never
sits down except for meals and not always then, because
"Mid-day meal goes on from 11.30 to 3, infants, school-
children and working sons". The copper for washing
is downstairs, but she nevertheless must do the washing
in her own rooms and hang it there when the weather is

wet. She is chronically short of money, because although she gets £3. 10. 0 from the working members of her family, she pays out of this 12/6 rent and 4/- for a room outside for two of the boys to *sleep* out, though they take their meals at her home. She has *no* leisure whatsoever.

Another terrific worker is Mrs. C. of Essex. She is 54, has had six children and one miscarriage and until eight years ago found that this family took up all her time, "especially as I should explain that I had my aged father and mother living next door and I had to run in and out all the time to attend to their meals". But as soon as her youngest child had left school she undertook "to help the District Nurse at confinements and anywhere else where help was required, and then running from door to door without waiting to put on a coat and loss of sleep made me rather ill and for two winters I was laid up with bronchitis". She now, however, is better again and, in addition to helping the Nurse and looking after one old parent still, she does the laundry work of four other families at her own cottage and goes out to housework for two hours a week. She is very cheerful and says she goes occasionally to the Pictures, reads a little, sews and knits, attends Women's Institute meetings, goes to local concerts and attends the Welfare Centre. She lives in a very inconvenient cottage, fetches all her water from the village pump and heats it on the kitchen fire.

As a last example of the wife of an unemployed man it is worth while to quote in full the answers given by Mrs. C. of Bolton. She is 39 and has had nine children and one still-birth. Four children have died and one is living away from home, so there are four at home now. The family of six live in a reconditioned clean cottage in an industrial part of the town. They have a bathroom, and they pay 7/6 rent. There is 28/- housekeeping money after rent is paid. Mrs. C. writes "I am constipated due to personal neglect. . . . I had albumen during pregnancy, I never knew the cause. I had has much rest as possible, and diet, doing without the usual foods—no salt, sugar pastry, meat, sweets. To bed early, rise not before 9 a.m. Light duties leaving off before feeling too tired. I attended the anti-natal clinic, had water tests plenty of good advice. I went to the Haslam Maternity home to have baby. Their I received the best attention and nursing Possible. Last year I had an attack of appendix because I ate a meat pie of which the meat was hard. I had hot formentations frequently untill the pain had completely gone, then warm flannels untill the Parts felt strong again. The Doctor advised an operation, said there may be a return attack, but I must risk that. Sometimes I feel to tired to go on. I believe it is the depressing times that is the cause of that spent feeling. I take half an hour for lunch, a little less for tea, after the little ones have gone to bed I can always find some mending, one night a week if it is fine I take a fairly long walk sometimes calling on a friend. Sunday night I like a good book. I beleive in plenty of plain green salads, and fruit. I never eat or drink between meals. I think it is a waste of time and altogether bad form. I try to get to bed at 10.30 as I must be up at 5.30 for 6.30 a.m. breakfast, and then to bed till 9. My house's work is not difficult to me, of course I do not possess the things that I should like. I am fond of cut glass, think the modern way of furnishing has done away with all difficult houswork. I was a Mill-worker before marriage (at 19) and before that I attended ordinary day school. We had drill several times a week and was taught that personal cleanliness was necessary for good health. I have gained much knowledge by attending the Child Welfare Centre with my babys".

Mrs. C. appears to have an excellent diet including salads and fresh fruit. The only tinned food she buys is milk and sardines.

Perhaps the most revealing expression of a wish is given by Mrs. N. of Woolwich who has seven children and lives in a tenement flat of four rooms, with "some bugs."

She has no water laid on in her flat, and a bad fireplace for cooking. She says that these are the chief drawbacks, but adds "I could also do with a Nursemaid"!

Adopted Children

Several women appear to have voluntarily adopted children—not grandchildren or the children of relatives, but only of friends. Mrs. C. of Rochdale is the wife of a plate-layer. She is 28 with two children of her own, and an adopted one of ten years old whose father and mother, now dead, were friends of hers. She is very anæmic and finds that her work gets "on top of me—when I am not feeling well, but I have no complaints".

Mrs. G. of Cardiff is 41, has had six children, three miscarriages and one still-birth. Two children have died. She adopted a child of five years old "as soon as I thought I wouldn't have any more". She is not at all well. She has had four operations for "stomache trouble" for which she now uses "hot formations". She also suffers from "Intestinal obstruction, very bad sight and headaches". She lives in a Council House, for which she pays 15/-. Her husband is an unemployed motor painter. Her only difficulties are in "rubbing and lifting".

CHAPTER VI

HOUSING

IT cannot be over-emphasised that the house is a mother's workshop as well as her home, and that, barring the occasional help of her husband and elder children in the evening or at weekends, the whole domestic labour is done by her. Since, as has been shown in earlier chapters, this absorbs most or all of her time, she has no change of scene, and for the most part, unless she can find pleasure in her house and work her life is infinitely dreary as well as arduous and monotonous. Every woman will do her utmost to make the home comfortable for her family when they come back from school or work. But if this has been achieved under the most difficult conditions and at the cost of unceasing toil the pleasure which husband and children find in such comforts as the house provides, is denied to her, who may be too exhausted to enjoy them, and whose only real relief would be an hour or two right away from the scene of her labour.

A few of these women express active enjoyment and pride in their home and housework, but these are nearly all in fairly good houses—Council houses or flats or clean old-fashioned villas, good cottages or adequate "rooms". For those in poor houses the most important thing in life is to get into another one.

Mrs. W. lives in Battersea, the street is dirty and noisy; she has had eight children of whom three have died and the family of seven is living in two rooms. There is one w.c. used by sixteen people. Mrs. W. is 34; her total housekeeping money is £2. 5. 0. from which she pays 7/6 in rent. She suffers from rheumatism, faintness and headache. The Health Visitor says "Her chief complaint is anæmia which she has not put down, caused I should say chiefly from post-partum hæmorrhage. She has had treatment from two hospitals, Battersea General, where she was an in-patient, and the South London Hospital for Women where she has had out-patient treatment though they wanted her to go in; she felt she could not leave the children. On her form Mrs. W. writes that she "had mastoid after confinement five years ago, it gathers inside the ear and makes headache". Her faintness she puts down to weakness through having the babies so quickly and "worry over the others who are none too strong". She writes separately the following poignant account of her present conditions:—

"I expect some people think living in 2 rooms one didn't have much work to do, I would rather clean a house down than clean my two rooms every day. I have a bed in the back for the two girls, a bed for the boy which I take down every day and put up at night to make more room, we have our food in this room I do all my cooking here; in the other room is my bed a bed I make up for the other little boy on the sette and the pram the baby sleeps in; I pay 7s. 6d. for these two rooms, I have a sheet board ceiling when it rains it runs halfway along this ceiling and then drips on the floor we have a bath in the middle of the room to catch the rain, over my bed it just comes in through the window frame on to the floor, the other room is the same, the back room has no proper grate sometimes it lets all the fire fall through into the hearth the front fire place when the wind is in a certain direction the fire and smoke comes right out into the room you have to put the fire out; the council people offered us a flat at 19/7 per week 2/- electric light how they think we could pay that out of 33/3 when my husband is out of work I don't know. I have just had my 8th baby who is a month old, he is bottle fed and not at all a strong baby, each one of my babies have been bottle fed as I am not strong enough to feed them myself, I have lost 3 one 11½ months one 5 weeks one 3 months 3 weeks three of the others have been in hospital for Heart trouble and Rheumatism one I paid 6/- per week for at Carshalton one I paid 4/- per week for at St. Stephens then he went to Bushy from the school, my husband being out of work they took the 2/– we were allowed from the Labour Exchange for his keep, the first baby I lost we paid 6/– in Fulham Babies Hospital for him when he went to St. James' we paid 5/– per week for him (then we were not in the H.S.A.) I have been in hospital for mastoid also attended for abcess under chin, we are always paying out for the children or for myself to some hospital or nursing home it dos'nt give one a chance to get on however much one try, my husband was only a labourer until he got a Bricklayer's ticket 2 yrs ago, when he is in work I can get along comfortably but there always seems to be something cropping up, I have a great deal to thank the welfare people for, they have been very good and kind to me both in giving me advise and helping me in trouble with the babies."

Mrs. W. of Brighton has recently moved into a new Corporation housing estate, and has four rooms and a scullery. She says she is in much better health since she moved. "Being up on the hill, the air seems to benefit me, also being near the sea I think does me good, and having a house one can breathe in. I am a small eater and the details I have given for food are what I usually have when my husband is in work. When out of work I do not have eggs or bacon, neither can I afford fruit and custard. I try to have vegetables, but we have to do with less meat. In summer I vary vegetables as I get them from the garden." Mrs. W. has been very anæmic, and her diet is not calculated to help this; but in spite of this she says "even the anæmia has been better lately, perhaps because I get out to help my husband on the allotment, or the birth of the last baby. I still have severe headaches but that is worry due to my husband's unemployment and slack times and how to make ends meet."

Although a higher rent will necessitate a terrible pinching in the food budget (the most elastic item in the family expenditure) this will be readily undertaken by such women as Mrs. W; a rent of 19/– however is, of course, out of the question. She would rather starve herself than have to continue to live and work in these conditions; and life would regain a little of its former brightness if she could get a home in which she could take some pride, even at the cost of her only square meal. It is not too much to say that while high food values may be of greater importance to the health of her husband and children than the kind of house they sleep in (for generally they spend many hours a day in another environment, in large airy rooms and in the open air), a good house is far more essential to the mother's wellbeing than a good diet.

Generally speaking, the housing conditions of these 1,250 women can be divided into three groups. The first are Council houses or flats, the older type of villa or well-built cottage, in a healthy position, and providing sufficient space for the family. If in a town there will be electric light, hot and cold water and either a small private garden or good playground for the children. Into this category may also be put those flats, not self-contained, lived in by a very small family, in a well-kept tenement house, where the main inconvenience is the lack of a private bathroom or W.C. Such families are generally in better financial circumstances than those with many young children and are therefore able to send out their washing thus avoiding the ghastly discomfort of inadequate sinks and, what is still worse, no drying facilities. There are some cottages in the country, not Council houses, which could also be put into this category. About 86 women or 6·9% of the whole number are living in this good type of house, comparatively adequate in size, moderately convenient and generally healthily situated.

But even houses and flats in this group have many disadvantages, and are often incapable of providing that standard of healthy environment or of home comfort which every human being should be able to command. They generally ensure a certain amount of privacy for the family as a whole, but it is extremely rare to find *within* the family the possibility of any privacy at all for any

of its members. The parents of small children almost certainly have one or perhaps two children sleeping in their room; and it is very rarely possible at any time in the life of the school child or the young unmarried worker to give him or her a bedroom to himself unless he is a member of a very small family. The following account comes from a Birmingham woman who feels very strongly about personal privacy; it gives an accurate picture of the home conditions of many an adolescent child in the better circumstanced among the 1,250 families under review:—
"Until I was 23 years of age, I lived with my Grandparents in a six roomed house. Until I was 15 conditions were fairly good. I shared a room with a young Aunt and there were my Grandparents in one bedroom and an Uncle in another. After I was 15 my Aunt got married and I had to have a bed in the same room as my Grandparents. For about a year my Grandfather was suffering from cancer and about two months of the time was a nightmare to me. I lay at night listening to him choking. . . . My Grandfather died when I was 18, after that I shared the room with my Grandmother and cousin (7 years). When I was 23 they tried to put another cousin in the room and then I left. Since then I had several lots of digs but each time had a room to myself; it was glorious, and I shall never forget it with my children, if only I can manage it somehow."
Here are some instances amongst these married women of the inconveniences of even the best sort of house. Mrs. S. of Woolwich is in a Council house, she pays 14/7 rent out of £2. 12. 6. housekeeping money. The house has four rooms and she has six children all under 13, the house lies low with a high railway embankment at the back and there is "a constant noise of trains". A woman living in a small market town in Essex with seven children (three boys and four girls) has a four-roomed Council house i.e. 3 bedrooms and a kitchen.[1] Her diet is atrocious

[1] The "standard" minimum 3-bedroomed house as recommended by the National Housing and Town Planning Council in 1929, was

and she suffers from severe constipation and headaches, but says she is quite content with her home conditions, and that they have no drawbacks. Mrs. Y. of Bolton who is comparatively well-off is buying her house by instalments. It has four rooms and she has three children over 15 living at home; this house has *no* bathroom and "a very dark larder built under the stairs, impossible for food". Two women in Council houses in Rotherham complain that the bathroom is downstairs near the back door and therefore very cold, and that the scullery is so small that they cannot hang their washing there and must put it to dry in the living room. One of these women has six children, both are very poor and are paying rents of 9/6 out of housekeeping money of 38/- and 40/- respectively. Several women complain that Council houses have cement floors which are "terribly cold for the children" unless they are thickly carpeted.

In an L.C.C. flat a woman who is paying 16/9 rent out of 41/- income (her husband has no employment except a newspaper round and he gives her all the money to manage) has three young children and six flights of stairs to climb up to her flat and to take the pram up and down, "but otherwise no complaints or drawbacks". She suffers from prolapsed uterus and bad anæmia and has had one miscarriage and one still-birth.

Another serious disadvantage of many Council houses is the distance from the wage-earner's work. Two women in Birmingham living on one of the Corporation estates on the outskirts of the city complain of the tram and bus fares for their husbands and sons. One of them has eight children, her housekeeping money is 40/- "only, because

---

adopted by the Government in 1932 and referred to by Sir Hilton Young as the type of house most needed, in the debate on the Housing Bill in December 1932. This house (of which the one in the market town of Essex is a sample) has a total floor area of 760 square feet,—380 square feet on each floor. This gives three bedrooms of approximately $12' \times 12'\,6''$, $10' \times 10'$, $9' \times 7'\,6''$; the rest, $63'$ is for landings, staircase, etc. The bathroom of such houses is downstairs.

of husband's bus fares 5/- a week," and she pays a rent of
10/6 out of this. A miner in Rochdale has a wage
of £2. 4. 3—four children—pays 8/1 rent and 3/6 in bus
fares.

Noise, again, is a serious drawback to many of the
best Municipal Housing Estates. A woman in a large block
of flats in West London complains bitterly of the noise from
the courtyard when the children of over 600 flats are playing
there. The flat is comfortable and roomy but she says
"there is never any quiet, especially in summer when the
children come home from school, sometimes I feel I would
rather have them on top of me or in the old street".

But on the whole these 86 women are fairly content with
their housing conditions. Mrs. C. of Stafford is in a new
six-roomed Council house and has eight children of whom
seven aged from 19 down to 7 years are living at home.
She says "As it is a new Council house there are no
difficulties. I find washing too heavy, of course, otherwise
I get through the work nicely". She works hard but is
well and happy and spends her leisure "reading, going for
walks or to Chapel". And again Mrs. R. of Fulham has
just moved into a new flat. She writes "I find the washing
and ironing rather fatiguing but I manage the rest of the
work quite well now that I have a flat of my own. Used
to live in two rooms and then found I was always tidying
up". The new flat has three rooms besides the living-
room-kitchen and a bathroom; six of the family live in
and two other children are boarded out. Mrs. R. has
"very good health, thank you".

It is interesting to notice that the standard of women in
good or fair houses gradually rises, and they begin to
complain about the lack of certain amenities which, in a
poorer house with far worse drawbacks, they would never
have noticed. Mrs. N. of Colchester is the wife of a motor
mechanic and they have recently moved into a "semi-
detached villa". She complains that her "sitting room
faces north; though I didn't used to notice that sort of

thing where I used to be, but it is a nice home". Mrs. L. of
Rotherham who lives in a "good class Municipal Housing
Estate" complains of "a dark, double-turning staircase";
presumably she feels that paying a rent of 15/1 out of her
housekeeping money of 50/– she is entitled to every luxury.
She has four children and works extremely hard, being
16½ hours on her feet. A woman in Leeds would like "a
bit of garden at the back for the children to play in, as
well as the piece in front where me and hubby can sit, but
suppose this too much to ask, and rent so moderate".
She does not say what her rent is but it is a Municipal
house so that presumably at the time of writing (1936)
she was benefiting by the excellent Leeds Rent Rebate
Scheme which was then in force. And it will be remembered
that a lady in Llanelly already quoted on page 84 com-
plained that she had nothing to cook on except an electric
stove ! And a superior young woman in Accrington, with
one baby, who goes to League of Nations meetings,
lectures and concerts, complains that she has "*no* electricity
and no refrigerator for keeping milk and food" ! She was
a mill-hand before marriage.

The second group of houses is the largest of the three.
They accommodate 771 of these families, i.e. about 61·6%.
They are poor houses but not slums even by a broad
definition of the term nor entirely incapable of being made
into tolerable homes. They can be kept decent by dint of
extremely hard work, and the housewife, as long as she is
strong and capable and able to maintain her courage, will
find some reward for the arduousness of her labour. These
houses have many serious inconveniences but not of the
worst and most irremediable kind such as are found in the
last and worst group. They are often over-crowded but
as has been seen this is usual even in the best working-
class houses; nor are they verminous and although they
are often in unattractive surroundings the streets are neither
unhealthy nor dingy. The rooms if in a town may be large
and well ventilated; if in the country, they may open out

on to a pleasant garden and have plenty of space and air; generally they are in tolerable structural condition. The multiple inconveniences from which they suffer are partly compensated for by rents which are mostly (though not always) much lower than those of the newer sort of house.

All this, however, is the brighter side of things. As far as the husband and children are concerned this type of dwelling can be and often is made into a fairly comfortable home. But from the woman's point of view it has every possible disadvantage and just because she feels that by hard work she can keep it fairly decent for her family, she struggles to maintain her standard and is more enslaved by her work than the women in either of the other groups. Every possible drawback exists to make her work harder and less pleasant. Far from there being any labour-saving devices the bare necessities of a decent existence may be extremely difficult to obtain. In cities like London and Liverpool, this type of house is exemplified by the tenement dwelling, "converted" from the old spacious though desperately inconvenient middle-class house built in the first half of the nineteenth century; there has, in fact, been no conversion. The house now occupied by four, five or six families is left exactly as it was when built for the occupation of one; sanitation, bathroom (if it exists at all), water supply, are all the same as were provided in 1840 for the single family, when the standards even of the rich in these respects were unhygienic and wasteful of labour; no labour-saving devices existed, for servants could be hired very cheaply to deal with the drawbacks. Now the working-class housewife living on an upper floor (which is undeniably more desirable and healthier than the basement) has probably to carry her clean water upstairs from the basement, or at the best from a tap on a mid-way landing, and carry it down again to be emptied. She may have to heat it on an open fire in a room which, once a pleasant bedroom or nursery, is now used as a living-room-kitchen and has no cooking stove; there may possibly be a gas ring. The baby's pram will have to be hauled up and down stairs so that it does not clutter up the dark and gloomy, but once dignified "hall". There is no possibility of an outside larder or decent cupboard in which to keep food; coal has to be stored in the sitting-room. There is no garden or courtyard in which to air the baby or to dry clothes. The W.C. which may be three flights down from the "flat", is shared by all the tenants of the house, and has to be kept clean by each tenant in turn. There is no privacy whatever; other people's noise, the smell of other people's cooking, the continual passing of other people's footsteps. However wide and well planned the street may be the noise and dirt and danger are ten times as great as they were 100 years ago. In fact just because the street is wide it will be much used for main traffic so that the anxious mother has to be continually on the look out for her children playing on the kerb. If she is sufficiently energetic after seven or eight hours' work before dinner she will take the younger children in the pram for an airing in the park during the afternoon, for probably there *is* a park in the neighbourhood of these Victorian family mansions.

Another type of house which comes into this category is of a smaller kind which is shared by two or possibly three families. It may consist of two floors only and having been built for the occupation of one family the only kitchen and scullery are on the ground floor and the two or three tenants agree to share these amenities. It is clear that to the careful and painstaking housewife this is a dreadful tribulation but a great many of the women in this group have to put up with this particular drawback. Noise and dirt are again disadvantages of this class of home. If the house is not one of the formerly respectable middle-class dwellings it is probably situated near factories from which there is endless dust and noise, or in a crowded main thoroughfare with trams and buses passing during twenty of the twenty-four hours.

In the country the type of house which has been placed in this group is the old inconvenient cottage which although it has an attraction of its own has certain very particular drawbacks. The rooms are probably small although "cosy", the windows are old and only one central pane is made to open so that there is insufficient ventilation to prevent dampness unless fires are constantly burning. Tap water is non-existent and water must be fetched, possibly from the village pump, a quarter of a mile away, or at the best from a well outside which may be shared by several cottages. There is no possibility of gas or electricity either for cooking or lighting and although washing facilities are very much easier than in the town houses above described, the copper is often removed from the house. There is the inestimable advantage of a garden in which not only the children can play, the baby can sleep, and the washing can be dried, but also vegetables can be grown. Even this, however, means extra work for the housewife, for she has to be constantly cleaning away muddy foot-marks. Sanitation though quite hygienic will consist of an earth closet and be situated at the end of the garden. It is, however, undoubtedly true that although the country woman has all these drawbacks to contend with she seems to get more time for leisure, is able to rest more, and often goes out to work for a few hours a week in the village in order to supplement her income.

Mrs. W. of Woolwich lives in four rooms on the two upper floors of a four-storey house; "the scullery in which I cook is on the ground floor and there is no pantry or bathroom which seems somehow to treble my work". There is one W.C. for the three families of the house. Mrs. W. has three children under ten, so her flat is not over-crowded. She can use the garden but it is two floors down. She pays 15/3 rent out of £2 15s. 0d. housekeeping money. She has had two miscarriages and one still birth.

Mrs. K. of Marylebone has two rooms on the top floor of a healthy old-fashioned house with large windows and "a feeling of space", she has four children and there are eight flights of stairs to the top of the house "but it is nice when you get there". The washhouse is on the ground floor and water is fetched from a tap on the second landing. One of Mrs. K.'s rooms is fitted as a kitchen and she has the use of a roof and of the yard on the ground floor. All the family goes regularly to Marylebone Baths. She suffers from nerves, headache and what she calls "heridetary raimatism" for which she finds salts and exercise the best remedy. She actually goes out to work for several hours a week, and says that her only household difficulties are the "worries and troubles of life generally".

Again Mrs. O. is in the same type of house in Paddington, only there are seven people in two rooms, for, by the age of 29 she has had five children. Her only complaint about the house is "not having a kitchen"! She appears to be quite well and according to the visitor "manages amazingly".

A country woman in Essex complains that her cottage is damp and that she has to keep fires going all day long, she has a whole string of ailments and finds that "wash days come very hard to me as I have no copper. All water to be fetched out of well which I share with neighbour and as house very draughty I cant keep warm". She has four children in a five-roomed cottage and a "nice piece of garden" so that it is not over-crowded.

Some of the worst complaints in this group are about the sharing of amenities. An East Sussex woman writes "On washing day as there is one copper between the four cottages I find work very hard and we each have to have our own day, mine being Thursday." A young woman in Birmingham aged 24 with one baby has two comfortable rooms for which she pays 9/- out of 36/- housekeeping money. She is the sub-tenant of the other occupants of the house and she shares with them the cooking stove and sink in their downstairs kitchen. Her food and coal have to be stored in her living-room and she complains bitterly of the lack of privacy. Actually, of course, this uncomfortable way of living is probably much healthier for the family than the same sized separate tenement would be, as the living room is kept free from the smell and steam of cooking and washing, but for the housewife herself it is an intolerable condition. Another young married woman in Croydon with one baby, had formerly been in good-class domestic service. She complains of "no privacy, kitchen used by dirty people, bath unusable and back yard filthy. One W.C. used by everyone in the house." Another woman in Croydon with one child is the wife of an unemployed statistical clerk and obviously is of superior education and intelligence. She lives in two rooms of an unconverted tenement house for which she pays 15/- rent out of 29/- housekeeping money. She has no sink and writes "It means running to the bathroom every time I want to fetch or empty water and as this is two floors down and I have a young baby it makes unnecessary trouble in the work".

And finally to give examples of the anxiety caused by the children having to play in the street; a woman in Birmingham writes "my greatest difficulty is in keeping the children off the street with heavy traffic, the house is in a congested area in noisy busy street, no garden, very small back yard, shared with others, and the children dont like playing here." A Rotherham woman shares a yard with thirteen other families and "so the children will go out of the front door which opens on to the main thoroughfare. Dangerous for children." Even a Council house in Rotherham has a yard common to four houses and a mother living in one of these says "Busy thoroughfare, road dangerous, no place for children to play. Playing field 200 yards away from house and am in continual fits when children go there." She has five children, the eldest being 6 years old.

The remaining 391 women, or 31%, live under the worst conditions of all, conditions which are completely intolerable, or rather which should not be tolerated by a civilised society. They include all the inconveniences of the last group but generally a greater combination of them in one house and in addition most of them are even more over-crowded and many are verminous. It is not surprising to find that, in such houses, the mother is easily discouraged; and as no amount of work can overcome these conditions she gives up hope and very often becomes slatternly and dirty herself. There are many tenement houses in this group like those described in the second group, but in which larger families are living, so that the inconveniences are much greater. Often the landlords are of the worst kind who avoid as far as the Local Authorities allow them, all responsibilities towards their tenants. There are also in this group those dwellings technically defined as slums, "radiating centres of depravity and disease";[1]—the old type of small working-class house in industrial areas built either round a narrow airless court-yard or straight onto the pavement of a long narrow dirty street. Such houses will share water supply, sanita-tion and such drying space as there may be for washing in a dirty passage at the back, or the aforesaid court, or even in the street itself. In the country although there is not here the lack of fresh air and space outside the house, the cottage itself may be in such bad condition as to be totally unfit for human habitation and it may be as vermin-ous and as over-crowded as the urban slum cottage. It will also have the usual country difficulties of fetching water from some distance, the distance from shops and schools and the inconveniences of lighting and heating. In such houses both in town and country it is not unusual to find that the ground floor windows do not open at all.

Many of the women in Glasgow are living in intolerably over-crowded conditions. There are in this city many tene-ments which consist of one room and a kitchen and amongst the families visited there a very large number were living in such homes. Glasgow women are on the

---

[1] Sir Hilton Young (later Lord Kennet) when Minister of Health.

whole good housewives and it is astonishing how well
they manage in this sort of accommodation Several of them
complain that they have to do their washing at the public
washhouse and that they don't like this especially of course
if it is some distance from the house, but it is at least
some consolation that they do not attempt to do this
part of their domestic work at home. In Liverpool for
instance a woman who is living with her husband and
five children in one room of "a large old respectable
house" has to fetch her water for all purposes from the
basement and all the washing is done in one room which
she says is "very inconvenient". Mrs. B. of S.E. London
lives also in "a large old-fashioned house"; she has two
rooms; she is 39 and has had nine children of whom three
have died, and five miscarriages. There are therefore eight
in the family including herself and her husband. She says
"the water has to be carried up three flights of stairs and
then all taken down again to be thrown away and there
is always so much washing to do. The children have to
be sent to school clean and fed three times a day." She
is anæmic, has varicose veins, headaches and piles; her
husband is out of work. Another woman in Croydon
lives in one room with her husband and eight children.
She has had ten children of whom two have died, and
one miscarriage. She writes that she has "no cupboards,
no stove only bedroom fireplace no chimney pot no water
on my floor." Her diet for herself is given as bread and
butter and tea only except on Sunday when she has "a
piece of meat for ten" and she adds "butter=marg. The
room is so full of beds it is difficult to clean it but I do
when it is wet the washing has to be dried in my only
room." She pays 3/6 for this home; and her husband
is a disabled sailor.

Another woman in Croydon has a six-roomed house
for which she pays 9/2 out of housekeeping money of
45/–. She has nine children, her husband and father to
look after. There is no back door to the house and refuse

has to be carried through the house to the dust cart; no bathroom or hot water, and she finds it very hard to keep clean. "No room to move all beds have to be big to accommodate children, no cupboards for clothes and I have no wardrobe, ground floor always dirty, children have to play in the street and come in and out by front door. Always tired with trying to make ends meet." She manages however to go out to laundry work occasionally. This woman has been married fifteen years and had her first holiday since then, at Littlehampton after the birth of her last babies (twins of one year), because she was in bed for five months with puerperal sepsis. She had a Home Help when she was "ill with the twins".

Another terrible case of over-crowding is at Deptford where there are six in one room. The father is consumptive and two children of 13 and 4 are in the Consumption Hospital. The mother says that her room is too small, and that she was taught at school to have plenty of fresh air ! She suffers from catarrh in the chest and head which she puts down to having "no proper footwear"; she has 29/6 housekeeping money.

That over-crowding can be nearly as bad in the country as in town is proved by Mrs. M. of Sussex who suffers from giddiness, headaches, and severe internal pain. She has five children; her husband is a carter on 45/- and she pays 7/2 rent for an old inconvenient cottage. She puts down all her aches and pains to worry "how to make sleeping accommodation for seven people including parents, two sons and two daughters between 10 and 17 and one daughter of 4 in two bedrooms". Again Mrs. B. is the wife of a labourer in Essex, she has three children under 5 and with the last pregnancy developed kidney trouble. Her cottage has two rooms only, is built of lath and plaster and is very low and damp. The investigator writes "She is a clean practical young woman, takes the children out as much as possible so as to be away from the house and manages her housekeeping money (26/-) very cleverly, fresh fruit and green vegetables are regular items in her diet, and she gets free milk from the local Child Welfare Centre (fortunately she is near one) during her last pregnancy and while nursing the baby. Her cottage is quite impossible."

As examples of bad sanitation we may quote a woman in Derby who lives in a house in a slum court entered through an archway in a slum street. The visitor says "She has no facilities for cleanliness at all. The surroundings are squalid, the houses jammed close together and the court very narrow, and festooned with unsavoury articles of clothing. At the end of the court is the row of tub lavatories shared with the other cottages. The Corporation clears the tubs twice a week. She gets water from a tap at the end of the yard." There is no sink in the house. This woman is 24, she has three children under five and is in very bad health. She has never been to the "Talkies". Another woman in Rochdale lives in a back-to-back house and all the sanitary conveniences, dustbins and lavatories, are two streets away.

Two women in Arbroath speak of the W.C. being shared between twenty-five and twenty-one people respectively. One of these has six children under seven and is again pregnant. She never eats eggs or fish, and only carrots or turnips in the way of vegetables. Her main dish is "stovies" made with onions, potatoes and water; she never puts either dripping or meat into them. Her only "ailment" is "having too much to do", and for this she does not take any advice but just "braves it off".

And now for the vermin. The wife of an unemployed labourer in Derby lives in a cottage where "The bugs which are present and breed in the rotting woodwork cause endless extra work in an endeavour to be clean. *It has been necessary to sit up at night to keep the bugs off the small baby.* The Corporation is said to have refused to fumigate the place at present. The job has to wait until the end of the slum clearance scheme." (Investigator's Report). The

woman has very poor health. She is "languid and weary
. . . husband has had two months work in 3 years. Difficulties connected with lack of money and a house infested
with bugs." She has about two hours, leisure (three
children). "Sit down no energy for walks no money for
pictures."

Mrs. R. of Llanelly has two rooms in a four-roomed
house. "It is rat infested, drain in the house, damp, dark
and low down and bugs in summer. I feel tired almost
every day since living in this house, and have headaches.
It is low and dark and think that has something to do with
headaches." She is 24 and has one baby and she pays 4/6
rent; her husband is unemployed. In Essex Mrs. E.
lives in an old cottage on a quay-side. She is 32
and has six children. Her rent is 7/2 and her husband is
a labourer on 35/–. The cottage has four rooms in all,
"the cooking range wont work and it has live-stock in
summer" (this is explained in another part as meaning
bugs and fleas). She suffers from "period pains, cute
constipation, lumbago, toothache and giddiness. I take
all kinds of Physic and try to regulate but with no avail."

There are literally dozens of cases in which the woman
expresses openly her discouragement about the house and
hundreds in addition to those quoted above in which it
is clear that no pleasure whatsoever is to be found in her
domestic work or home conditions. The wife of an Essex
labourer speaks of her cottage as being "300 or more
years old, damp low and the floors upstairs are all uneven.
I work and work all day and then at the end I cannot see
what I have done." A woman at Woolwich who lives with
her husband and two children in one room paying 5/–
rent says, "In spite of our home being so small I get no
rest. It is a one room home therefore cannot make nice
home. Girl of 4½ shares our bed. Suits husband all right
as he doesn't want to pay more rent. But I went to the
Health Exhibition at the Town Hall, which I thought
lovely especially the model houses." Another woman

living in an old London cottage in the East End for which she pays 12/6 rent says, "I have lost interest in my house because so dilapidated and never looks clean and tidy because never done cleaning it." She has six children and suffers from dyspepsia, breathlessness and acute depression.

The woman at Thornton Heath with seven children, who has been fully quoted on pp. 50 affords a good example of the disheartening effects of bad housing conditions and the inevitable deterioration in health which follows. Her long and carefully moderate account bears witness to her courage and good sense; but it is clear that she has lost all pleasure in her work, and that the drawbacks of her house contribute enormously to her depression and weariness.

And here is a woman in Rochdale, Mrs. J., who has become almost hysterical in her horror of the conditions in which she lives. The house is in a back street facing back doors, the street is a cul-de-sac. "There are plenty of drawbacks, over-crowded, dirt back and front as we have no back door, damp floors, damp walls, no convenience, walls and floor leaving each other." There are a living room, scullery, and two bedrooms, for a family of eight; the children are three boys, the eldest of whom is 15, and three girls the eldest being 12. Mrs. J. has £3 10s. 0d. housekeeping money and the rent is 5/6. She suffers from headaches, nerves and bad rheumatism. As the cause of these she writes "not enough fresh air, defective sight through house being very dark and always having gas lit when it rains or is dark through depression outside. I wear glasses but I think I should be better if I was in different surroundings. No outlook only into a yard, full of nothing but dustbins and W.C.'s and rubbish and a house that gets on your nerves through never being able to keep it tidy owing to the surroundings and children always getting colds through sleeping in damp rooms and being confined and cramped. I have tried different things but will never be any better until some fresh accommodation is found as I have tried for about 8 or 9 years to get a fresh house but cannot get one when you say you have children. Advice is no use it is a house I want with comforts. It is a wonder I dont go off my head with worry how to keep the place. I have had my teeth extracted for a safeguard against poison on the clinic doctor's advice about 12 months ago but cannot get any more false ones as it is a trial getting remidies for the children to keep them well with the way we have to live in this terrible house. My husband has been to the housing committee for a house but the manager and clerks tell him nothing can be done as we are not in a condemned area but better houses have been closed than ours never mind being overcrowded. There is only one way out of the place each time we go out or come in we have to pass 11 W.C.s and 11 ash bins and 3 or 4 open grates over drains, it is a dirty back it has never been paved only about a yard in front of the houses, whenever we go to our door and look out all we can see is about half dozen W.C.s and ash bins always when you sit down to enjoy a meal someone from a back door opposite will come out and flush the W.C. or throw something in the ash bin they have no back yards so it is not very private we have to join W.C.s with our next door neighbour so sometimes you go or the children want to do their business it is occupied by someone so they must wait, which is not good for anyone much less children." Is life not difficult enough without the humiliation and misery to which two such women as this one and Mrs. W. of Battersea quoted at the beginning of this chapter, are unnecessarily subjected?

As to rent it can safely be asserted that amongst the people who are under consideration the rent is nearly always too high. It is quite usual to find it about 25% of the total income and not infrequent that it is one-third of the income. But even in those places where it is as little as 2/6 or 3/– a week, for instance in the old type of country cottage, which may represent only 10% of the income, the workers who live in such houses are so low paid that even this rent leaves far too little over to supply the basic necessities of life.

It has been said that rent in its relentlessness is the tap root of poverty and it is certain that not only its mathematical relation to income but also its inelasticity makes it the worst of all financial burdens and adds incalculably to the housewife's difficulties and distress of mind in trying to solve the eternal puzzle of expenditure and income.

Unless the housewife has reached the state of distress exhibited in the account given above by Mrs. J. of Rochdale and by others earlier in this chapter the tendency is to keep rent as low as possible especially if the income varies a great deal as it does in some cases. For instance, a Birmingham woman with several grown-up children has housekeeping money varying from £2 10s. 0d. to £4 10s. 0d. when all are working but only spends 5/– on rent. The cottage is too small and has no conveniences whatsoever, but she says, "I dont dare to look for a dearer house although it would make me much happier because I never know how much money is coming in." And another woman in Preston speaks of similar difficulties and says, "I have been offered a better house but the rent was double this one (that is 12/7 as against 6/6) and as the family is in and out of work I feel I dont know what to do."

Undoubtedly the rents charged in the Council houses both in town and the country are the most equitable of all in relation to the accommodation provided and this in itself gives some satisfaction to the occupants; but the difficulty in paying the rent, or rather in providing the means of life after the payment of the rent, is so great for many of the tenants of such houses that unless further rent assistance can be given the Council houses must fail to secure for the families who live in them the better standard of health and comforts for which they are designed; and they will continue to remain out of reach of the families. For instance, Mrs. L. of Devonshire, whose husband is an agricultural worker on 35/– a week and who has nine children is paying 10/– for a Council house. The visitor writes, "They lived before in a back-to-back house which was badly ventilated, very dark and unfit for living in. They now have a garden to grow vegetables, but it is small wonder the mother is badly constipated and very anæmic. She tells me she buys all the food for under £1 a week." This woman has taken the plunge in spite of her poverty; probably because she felt she could not stand her old house any longer; but it has been at the cost of nutrition. Another woman in Sussex is paying 13/– for a five-roomed Council house out of £2 10s. 0d. housekeeping money. She has four children and says that her difficulties are in "making ends meet. Very difficult to keep rent and insurances going and in winter, when extra coal is required, I get worried to death about food." But there are hundreds of women who, even were the houses available at present rents, would not take on the extra financial burden in their existing circumstances.

In houses other than Council houses the rent is often higher and the accommodation of course much less good. For instance, in Fulham Mrs. R. is paying 18/– rent out of a total income of £2 14s. 0d. for three small rooms and a scullery. She says the flat is damp, the house is old, the ceilings low, and the steam cannot get away. Mrs. R.'s budget is given at the end of the next chapter. The woman in Croydon who is paying £1 for a damp, dark flat with outside sanitation has already been quoted above. A woman in Hampstead who lives in a "lower middle-class street and a semi-basement flat" complains of the lack of privacy and that the boiler which serves the whole house is in her living-room and makes it very hot. She pays 25/– for this out of housekeeping money of £3. Mrs. Y. of Rotherham whose husband is unemployed receives 28/9 for housekeeping money and is paying 12/– rent for an old house with no garden, very dark and opening straight on to the main street. And a woman in Accrington who is obviously very proud of her house as she says it is "pallasaded, self owned (by which she obviously means self-contained) property, very superior", has 35/– a week housekeeping and pays 10/– rent. She remarks that she has no scullery or bathroom and only a tiny garden (presumably behind the palisade). A very intelligent woman in Cardiff who has been quoted before (page 36) has 25/– left after paying 18/– for her rooms in a large old house. She has five children, herself and her husband to keep, the eldest boy having only one leg. Another woman in Accrington who lives in "a long row of small garden houses, with a very small garden at the front of the house" complains of the extra work caused through dirt and soot from a factory chimney immediately behind the house. She pays 15/– rent out of total housekeeping money of £2.

These examples are chosen from many hundreds of the same kind and show clearly what an impossible burden rent is upon the income, for a large majority of working-class families. The largest, who are generally the poorest families, cannot really *afford* any rent at all. It is they who need the better house most, but who seldom can get one at the rent which they can just manage to pay.

The routine of housework would form an interesting subject of investigation. There is little doubt that it suffers from a rigid conservatism which is not caused entirely by the absence of modern conveniences, or inadequate equipment and utensils. Even with such difficulties to contend with those women who use their brain in planning their work get more leisure, are better in health and take obvious pride in their own efficiency. But too often the fight against irremovable difficulties is so hopeless that the woman gives up trying to plan even with such resources as she has. She just gets on with the job immediately under her hand, as best she can without thinking of how it can be fitted into a regular time-table. The wonder is not how little but how much she achieves with so many odds against her; not how dirty but how clean she manages to keep herself, her family and house; not how depressed but how

cheerful she remains. One is tempted to ask why, if water
has to be fetched from a yard or heated in a kettle, is
washing-up done after every meal ? Or, why, when cooking
facilities are poor, fuel expensive, and other work abundant,
is cooking performed every day instead of two or three
times a week ? The answers to such questions are implicit
in the accounts these women give of their household difficulties. There is very seldom crockery and cutlery enough
for more than one meal and therefore it must be washed
up before the next meal. Besides, as the kitchen is also
the living-room, the sight and smell of greasy dishes would
obtrude themselves during the woman's next two or three
hours of work. There is no place to store food cooked or
uncooked, nor utensils to store it in, and even if the
saucepans, etc., were adequate where could a woman put
them so that they would be out of her way ? One woman
showed the investigator with pride a new coal bin made
by her husband to stand in the living-room. Inside the
bin and fixed on the back, were two small shelves upon
which all her cooking utensils were stored. When the visitor
exclaimed that they must get covered with coal dust the
woman replied, "Oh, I dont mind that, I can wash that
off before using them. You see they are out of my sight
and I can make the room like a sitting-room." In another
case the visitor commented on the gay wallpaper in the
living-room particularly on its attractive shaded effect.
The housewife's eyes filled with tears as she said that she
and her husband had put it up less than a month ago and
the "shading" was where the colour had run owing to
the steam and the damp in the room "mostly on washing
days but some of the time every day". This is a Paddington
house in a dingy little street of houses built straight on to
the pavement, the family occupies the two ground floor
rooms,—father, mother, four children and a very large
dog ! The kitchen (in which was the blotched wallpaper)
is 9 ft. square; the other room about 11 ft. by 10 ft. The
mother said she was lucky in having three girls and the

youngest, a boy of 6. The three girls could sleep in the front room and the boy in her own double bed with herself and her husband. This bed took up one-third of the total kitchen space and was used *as the table at meal times*. When the visitor suggested that the feeding of the dog must be a great difficulty, the mother replied that nothing would ever persuade her to part with him because he was her children's chief plaything. He was obviously much better fed than the mother herself.

One of the many domestic worries of women in these circumstances is lack of furniture and the payment for such as exists. Hire Purchase is continually mentioned in these 1,250 forms as a regular item of the household budget, the most usual figure given being 3/– a week. It is not rare to find bitter complaints of the quality of the furniture that is being bought on this system; and as all these accounts were given before the passing of Miss Wilkinson's Bill, it is certain that a great many of the women suffered from manifold injustices in this respect.

Another difficulty is when the husband or sons are doing night shifts of work and have to sleep during the day in the rooms in which other members of the family are eating, working or playing. Many mothers speak of the disorganisation of their work through such a cause, and it is again a reminder of the irony of the life led by people of this social stratum. Regular night work is practically unknown to persons of the upper middle classes, who would anyhow have the accommodation which would ensure proper rest for the worker and an easy adjustment of the housework for the housewife or her domestic staff. But nightwork in the small wage earner's home is a nightmare for the mother, and an impossible hardship both for the night worker himself and for his family. He can get no proper rest, and the family no enjoyment of the few amenities of their home.

The general conclusion to be drawn from the reading of these 1,250 accounts of the woman's life and work, is that a house in which she can take pride and pleasure (and every housewife has the right to be house-proud) is the greatest benefit which can be bestowed upon her, and the one for which she most ardently longs. Unless she is of the severely provident type she will cheerfully face the higher rent of a better house with all the extra scheming and calculations and close spending that it will entail. Physically and mentally the husband and children are not as sensitive to conditions of housing in their homes as might superficially be expected.

The fact that school medical officers have remarked upon the deterioration in physical fitness of children who have moved from bad to good housing conditions, is a proof that the lower standard of diet necessitated by a higher rent is not off-set by the healthier home environment, better conditions of rest, better ventilation, more open space round the house, etc. etc. This must be due to the fact that however bad the home conditions, the children spend very little of their time there, and do get fresh air and space for a great deal of the day. It is, however, easily intelligible that a change to better surroundings in her home should have a far greater significance for the mother, both from the point of view of health and of happiness. Even when she was spending less on rent, she did not eat much, and the new home will probably make very little difference to the actual amount she eats. On the contrary, although she will spend less on food for the whole family, the possibility of enjoyment in her work, of less smell and steam and bad air in her kitchen, will give an edge to her appetite, and even if she eats no more than before, her food will nourish her better. Unfortunately, the possibility of better housing conditions comes often too late to make much improvement in her health at all likely, and in many respects her work may be as hard, if not harder, in a better house than it was in the bad one. She probably has more rooms to clean, and the fact that she is proud of the house will encourage her to increased effort. But for all that she will be very much happier, and will have a far keener *sense* of well-being than she dreamt was possible before. Over and over again the women of this investigation have expressed this feeling of comparative ease and comfort when they speak of having recently removed from a bad to a good house, just as in the quotations given earlier in this chapter others who are still in bad houses have openly attributed their ill-health and depression to their horrible home conditions.

There is no reform which from the woman's point of view is of greater urgency than the immediate provision of enough decent houses at rents which the working-classes can afford. That women living in the conditions described by Mrs. J. of Rochdale above, and obsessed, as she is, by the horror of it all, should be denied a better house, is a devastating indictment of the national housing policy, or lack of it, during the last twenty years. No family, however large and however poor, should be unable to live in a pleasant home, any more than it is unable to receive a free and decent education. That reading and writing, important as they are, should have been granted priority over shelter, food and warmth, in the services given by the State to those citizens who are unable to buy these amenities for themselves is one of the strangest anomalies of modern civilisation.

CHAPTER VII

DIET AND THE HOUSEHOLD BUDGET

AFTER rents—what next? Fuel, light, insurances, boots and clothing, cleaning materials, household utensils and furniture. Some of all these a housewife must have, and therefore a certain amount of money must be put aside for them before food comes into the picture. What is left over she can then proceed to spend on food.

There is no need to attempt to prove that most of these women are under-nourished. In the last few years much scientific investigation has been devoted to the ideal food budget, and the nation as a whole is now "nutrition-conscious". It has been shown by the best authorities that a large part of the population is too poor to buy enough of the kind of food necessary for the maintenance of sound health. No unemployed married man with a family under the Assistance Board, nor any married man in such poorly paid trades as agriculture, receives enough money to buy adequate food for himself, wife and children.[1] The Public Assistance Committees, which are now the destitution authority, vary very much from place to place in granting additional relief; but whatever the policy adopted, it can safely be said that the standards

[1] When Part II of the Unemployment Act was under discussion in the House of Commons (December 1933) it was stated by the Minister of Labour (Sir Henry Betterton,—later Lord Rushcliffe) that the rates of assistance would be adequate to meet all needs other than medical needs. "The limit of need will not be confined in any way to the rate of unemployment benefit. It will be possible for the Board (i.e. the Unemployment Assistance Board) to supplement benefit in the case of persons under Part I and they will also be able to meet the whole needs other than medical needs to the extent that the meeting of those needs requires." Hansard, December 5th, 1933, col. 1615.

of relief are never such as to enable an average family to be properly fed.

It would be fantastic to judge the diets possible to any except about a dozen of these 1,250 families by any of the authoritative standards of food values which have been compiled in recent years. Whether the standard of measurement be (*a*) Sir John Orr's, (*b*) that of the British Medical Association, (*c*) Professor Mottram's, or (*d*) Mr. Rowntree's "Poverty Line",[1] the incomes of all but a very few of these women fall wildly short of what is required for basic nutritional needs.

It is probably true that better nourishment would be possible, even with the income she has, if the housewife exercised a more scientific choice of food, e.g. if meat were replaced by cheese, and if there were greater knowledge about the cooking and preparation. But given the lack of education, lack of time and lack of information about markets, and the appalling shortage of facilities and domestic conveniences, it is astonishing that she manages to keep the souls and bodies of her family together, let alone her own. The poor are made poorer still than appears from their "paper budget", by the additional practical difficulties of their situation; and the value of the sum available for food is depreciated in proportion to the difficulties attendant on the adequate preparation of meals. A large family (which is the chief ground of poverty) means more crowded accommodation and therefore less space for cooking and preparing a meal and for eating it. The room which

[1] (*a*) 10/- a week income per head; this being the lowest at which a diet can be adequate in quality and quantity.

(*b*) At present food prices about 7/- for a man's food (less for a woman or child).

(*c*) 5/1 a week for an adult's food.

(*d*) 41/3 for a man, wife and three children, 9/- being allowed for rent. This means 32/3 "housekeeping money" on the basis used by this enquiry, which equals 6/5 a head.

It should be noticed that all these scales are based on the assumption that every penny is spent to the best advantage, and that the housewife can always buy in the cheapest market, which is far from being the case in reality.

might be adequate for cooking for three people is insufficient for eight; and yet with the family of eight the
kitchen will be no larger than that of the small family.
It will contain more furniture—often a bed. It also means
that utensils are less adequate in kind and in number and
the necessary minimum takes up more room and uses
more hot water for washing. The absence of a sink which
is far commoner when the family is large, is a far worse
handicap. And lastly the time, care and forethought
required for the most economical use of her resources
are a far greater tax on the mother's strength and ingenuity.
Poverty therefore increases the housewife's difficulties in
relentless geometrical progression and it is not surprising
to find that she takes one comparatively easy way out by
eating much less than any other member of her family.
By saving the necessity to plan for herself, the difficulties
of the budget are somewhat lightened. Moreover, her
weariness at the end of a hard morning's work, the steam
and heat and smell in a small kitchen, combine to take
away her appetite. To serve her family she has to be
standing about a great deal and therefore finds it easier
not to sit down to eat, which means that she cannot eat
a hot dish properly. The alternative is to wait until the
family has finished, and then to sit down to eat whatever
"scraps that may be left".

In many hundreds of these 1,250 interrogatories the
woman speaks of going without herself for any or all of
these reasons. Health Visitors' accounts also speak of
the deplorable extent to which the woman will starve
herself in order that her children should have a little more
or that her labour should be lightened. Nor is this changed
even at the times when, for the sake of a coming child
as well as for herself, she should be getting a good diet.
It is well known that the unborn baby takes what it needs
from its mother so far as such requirements can be found
in her body; therefore it is the woman's reserves of nutri-
ment and vitamins which suffer during the nine months of

pregnancy, if her diet is inadequate.[1] It is clear that such extra food as the mother can get at these times through the various Social Services is totally inadequate to build up even in nine full months her already depleted strength. If the foundation is poor, the house cannot be imposing.

Mrs. G. of Newcastle, for example, who is 29, has been married ten years, has three children and has also had one miscarriage. Her youngest baby is 4 months old. Her husband was out of work until after the baby was born and she found it impossible to get proper food while pregnant. As a result partly of this she was very ill three days after the confinement and was then taken to hospital where she spent seven weeks. She came home for a week but had to return to hospital for an operation, and though she was at home at the time of filling in her form she was still in bed and the doctor and nurse were in daily attendance. She says that while she was pregnant she went out charring every day in order to increase the family income. She received extra milk at the Ante-natal Clinic from the fifth month of pregnancy but otherwise her diet was almost entirely bread and butter and tea with potatoes *or* mince meat *or* pudding at dinner time. She had an egg once a week and no vegetables except potatoes and occasionally turnips.

Mrs. M. of Fulham is 45 and has six children. She

[1] It is interesting to compare the provision made by the State for the care of women in pregnancy with the recent experiment carried out at Aldershot on sub-standard recruits by Captain P. J. L. Capon, R.A.M.C. (See Journal of the R.A.M.C., May 1937). Thirty-three recruits were taken on trial who were judged by the doctor to be capable of being made fit by proper food and exercise administered scientifically and intensively. Final standards of admission to the Army were modified as much as possible, and certain localised defects which did not affect general health were overlooked, e.g. flat feet were passed in a man who was destined for a mechanised unit. Out of the thirty-three recruits twenty-four were made fit in three months at a cost, *in addition to the ordinary Army allowance*, of 7/6 per head a week for *food alone*, bought as only the Army can buy at the most advantageous prices. Moreover, the recruits were during this time leading extremely healthy lives, with plenty of rest, fresh air and gentle exercise !

pays 17/6 rent out of an income "which sometimes reaches £2 17s. 0d. when husband working". She suffers from indigestion which she puts down to rushing over her meals; and from toothache for which she has had most of her teeth extracted. The Health Visitor writes: "This family have been badly off for two years while father was unemployed. The youngest child has been having a pint of milk daily supplied by the Borough Council and they bought one pint themselves also a tin of condensed for puddings. They get about six lbs. of greens and nine lbs. of potatoes weekly. We have a very cheap market where these can be had fresh every day. They also get a fair amount of fruit from the same source. The meat paste is bought by the lb. from the grocers. If anyone goes short it is the mother here of course." This woman also went out charring until the sixth child was born, and says she "mostly" feels well now—"but seldom when pregnant".

A country woman in Sussex who has three small children and is expecting another says "husband's work very uncertain, when on unemployment list, cannot get enough nourishing food for self and three young children, therefore I go without some things myself". She has an average of 30/- for housekeeping out of which she pays 6/- rent. She never has more than one egg a week unless they are very cheap and very few vegetables although she has a small vegetable garden of her own. Tinned fruit is looked upon as a luxury and is a Sunday treat. She has always been anæmic and suffers now from chronic constipation and debility, due she thinks to undernourishment; she is "sometimes given extra food from the Parish".

Mrs. C. in Woolwich is 34 and has two children. She spends 10/- on rent out of total housekeeping money of £1 17s. 0d. She suffers from gastritis for which the doctor wants her to go to hospital but she cannot leave the children; also from neurasthenia and high blood pressure for which she has been prescribed a meatless diet and abundant fish and milk. She says she cannot afford this and in consequence her dinner is mashed potatoes and gravy *or* milk pudding "made mostly with tinned milk". Another case where special diet is required comes from Woolwich as well. This woman is 32 and has had six children all under nine. She pays 15/- rent out of house-keeping money of 45/- and her mother-in-law lives with the family. She had albuminuria before the birth of the last baby and now suffers from high blood pressure, giddiness and indigestion. The Health Visitor writes "Her food is quite insufficient owing to the claims of the family and the giddiness is probably due to want of food. She has very bad teeth but has not the time or the money for hospital. She is a very conscientious mother." The woman states that she has "no time for dinner on Monday".

A Mrs. C. in Essex who pays 3/- rent out of 25/- for housekeeping money has three children to keep. The Health Visitor writes "She is very clean and a very good mother spending most of the housekeeping money on suitable food for the children and often goes without proper food for herself when she has had doctor's bills to pay for illness or anything extra". She has suffered from anæmia since the birth of her first child seven years ago which she puts down to "loss at confinement and lack of money to continue medicine" (this refers to an iron tonic given to her by the Welfare Centre for two months) but the Health Visitor says "It is clearly lack of proper food." Another mother in Newcastle is 30 years old and has four children and has had three miscarriages in eight years of marriage. She suffers from anæmia, faintness and chronic constipation. The doctor and Welfare Centre have advised her to have cod liver oil and malt which she gets "occasionally when able to afford it". She never touches fresh milk except in a milk pudding once a week and her fresh vegetables consist of potatoes and occasional turnips. The whole family (six people) live in two rooms and seven families use the W.C. This housewife has to carry water up two flights of stairs and to carry it down again to be emptied.

And lastly Mrs. D. of Liverpool subsists entirely on tea and toast and margarine with an egg at week-ends and a kipper twice a week. She has had fifteen pregnancies of which two were still-births and two children died from pneumonia. There are nine children living at home. The husband is mostly away being a "Seafarer". She pays 15/– rent for her seven room house and her total income is £3 8s. 0d. She goes out charring "as I couldn't possibly manage otherwise". She suffers from rheumatism for which she rubs on an ointment; kidney trouble for which she was in hospital six weeks but "couldn't stay longer owing to the children at home", and anæmia for which she takes Doctor William's pills. The Visitor says "I sometimes wonder to see Mrs. D. alive at all, her children range from 19 to 4½ and as far as I can see she never rests or eats".

Besides the financial difficulty of supplying adequate food for herself there is the one of the work being so hard that the housewife is too tired to eat. Many cases like this are mentioned. For instance, Mrs. G. in Essex lives in an old cottage which stands alone in about an acre of waste land. She has to carry water from a well a quarter of a mile distant and the garden is not made. She says that her husband is a labourer but the Health Visitor states that he is more often unemployed but does not spend the time he might in helping his wife. They have ten children and there has also been one miscarriage. Mrs. G's housekeeping money is £2 16s. 0. (which includes a small disablement pension for her husband,) of which 8/6 goes in rent. She says that she is too tired to eat herself although obviously she is a good manager as far as the children are concerned. She keeps a goat so that the family can have fresh milk. She has suffered from anæmia for fourteen years and says she takes no remedy. She adds "out of housekeeping money of £2 16s. 0d. there are two sows and their babies to be feed". And Mrs. A. of Glasgow who is quite well off gives her family of eight children an excellent diet according to the Health Visitor but cannot eat herself as she is so exhausted by the time she has prepared the family meals. She suffers from fatigue, shortness of breath and palpitation, and continual pain in the back. She is also awaiting an operation for an internal injury which occurred after the birth of the last baby seven years ago. She eats nothing except oatcake and tea and butter, very little fresh vegetables and only one egg a week. She gets up at 6.0 and goes to bed at midnight. In addition to the eight living children two have died and she has had one miscarriage. The Health Visitor adds that she has had puerperal fever once and has been treated as an out-patient for anæmia and gynæcological trouble.

As examples of sheer poverty where the supply of a good diet even for the family is completely impossible, the following may be given. Mrs. W. of Croydon has ten children living at home and pays 10/6 rent out of £2 housekeeping money. Her house has four rooms which she says laconically are not large enough. Her husband is unemployed but three of the children contribute a little towards the housekeeping money. The only variation in her diet of tea, bread and butter is "an occasional stew". Mrs. C. of Bermondsey has eight children, all under 14. Her housekeeping money varies from 30/- to £2 as her husband is a casual labourer. She has "bread and marg" for breakfast and tea, boiled potatoes for dinner and no supper at all. She says she is perfectly well. The whole family of ten people live in three rooms. Mrs. S. of Rhondda has had nine children and three miscarriages. She pays 12/6 rent out of housekeeping money of 44/-. She says also that coal costs her 2/-, clubs 2/-, furniture 2/-, which leaves her 25/6 for the needs of her family of eleven. Her own diet consists of bread and butter (or as she calls it "beard and butter") and on Sunday a little meat for eleven. She never eats eggs or fish and only a little vegetables on Sunday. She says she has "not suffant blood".

Mrs. N. of Rotherham has six children under 14 and pays 9/5 rent out of housekeeping money of 42/6. She drinks a great deal of tea, has an imported egg twice a week, a bit of fish about once a month, no supper and for the rest a slice of bread and marg. She says "with having 6 children to look after it is difficult to get through my work. My husband has been out of work 4 years and with having little money it is a great big trouble knowing how to spend it". She says also that the house is in a congested district and is damp and that the fireplace is broken so that she "can only cook in the oven". Mrs. T. of Liverpool has only two children but also has had two miscarriages in four years of marriage. She pays 11/2 a week out of 29/- housekeeping money. She eats "bread and marg", tea with condensed milk, one egg a week and occasionally carrots or turnips. She suffers from headaches, chronic constipation and piles and bad rheumatism. The Health Visitor says "She looks in very poor condition, she says she always feels tired and disinclined to do anything. I think she was probably not very strong before marriage, and four pregnancies in four years have drained her vitality. She attends the Clinic with the baby and gets a tin of food every two weeks but has not disclosed the fact that she is still breast-feeding as this is contrary to their advice". Mrs. T. herself says that she finds it impossible "to feed and clothe four people on such a small amount of money, clothing practically impossible".

In the country, poverty is to a small extent mitigated by having a garden, and however bad the diet may be in other respects, generally fresh vegetables appear every day. Occasionally too a few hens will be kept which make eggs a possibility. But it is noticeable that the women often say that as their children do not like greens they do not cook these for themselves and it is not unusual therefore to find the country diet as bad in this respect as that of any town dweller. If there is any particular ailment which needs special diet it is as difficult to supply it in the country as in the town. Mrs. D. of Durham has six children aged from 16 years to 8 months and pays 8/6 rent out of 37/6 housekeeping money, her husband is an unemployed miner and works hard on a small allotment outside the village. The family have fresh vegetables on three or four days a week, onions, salad and tomatoes appear often in the diet. Mrs. D. says "I have taught the children to like these and it saves so much money". She is a splendid manager and although her house has every possible disadvantage she says she manages to get through her work very well. There is no bathroom or scullery or indoor sink. She suffers from an inflamed eye, bad rheumatism, decayed teeth and prolapse of uterus.

In Devonshire several women speak of having vegetables every day and apples from their own trees. They are able, therefore, to make jam and fruit tarts. These women also get rabbits very cheaply. Of one Devon woman the Health Visitor writes "This mother has been very ill and the diet given is what she is allowed to eat. Her housing conditions are now good but very poor for many years when the children were young, poor ventilation and poor lighting etc. As the family was large and the income small she got in a very run down condition owing to lack of proper nourishment and I fear she will now never regain her strength". This woman is 58 and has had ten children. When they were young she worked as a "buncher" in flower gardens and found her work altogether too hard; she used to get up between 4 and 5 a.m. to get breakfast for her husband and she says "it is easy enough now with a daughter at home to look after me, but not in younger days when bringing up a family of 10 on £1." She suffers from nervous debility, fibrous tumour, loss of weight and has had pleurisy three times.

That some women are able under these or similar conditions to provide good food for their family is little short of miraculous. It is noticeable that the Scots and women from the north of England are better managers than those in the south. Mrs. S. of Glasgow who is 32 has four children and has had one miscarriage. Her husband is a steel-window fixer and she lives in the usual "self-contained flat of one room and a kitchen" and suffers from osteomyelitis of femur due to pleurisy and a miscarriage and in consequence does not feel well. She pays 5/4 rent out of 38/- housekeeping and says that she eats a lot of vegetables, eggs "often if cheap" and fresh fish. She is one of the few people who say they make vegetable and bone soup as she believes this is much more nourishing than meat and is a good deal cheaper. She gets two hours, leisure in the day and spends these either in the Women's Club or in the park according to the season. Mrs. T. of Newcastle has seven children living at home; she has had ten, and one miscarriage. She pays 9/9 rent out of an average of 31/- housekeeping money. Onions, carrots, barley, oatmeal and white puddings occur in her menus. She gets up between 5 and 6 a.m. and goes to bed between 10 and 11 p.m. and says that she is in splendid health. Mrs. M. of Birmingham is 35 and has had six children. She pays 6/5 rent out of 36/- housekeeping money and feeds nine people on the remainder "after clothing, insurances and cleaning utensils provided for"; (her mother-in-law lives with them). Cheese and tripe and beer occur in her own diet. She says she has fresh vegetables every day, an egg three times a week and fresh fish once a week. She lives in a back-to-back house of two rooms with no hot water and no garden. Nineteen people use the W.C. She says she feels perfectly well.

Mrs. M. of Rotherham is 30 and pays 8/- rent out of 30/- housekeeping money. She has six children and says that her husband "has been on short for a long period and it is a struggle to keep up payments". She seldom has tinned foods as she finds "they are too expensive, one tin of anything not being sufficient for the family". She has fresh fish three times weekly, fresh vegetables every day and occasionally eggs. Another woman in Rotherham aged 27 pays 8/3 rent out of 38/-. Her husband is out of work and she has six children. She makes her own bread and drinks fresh milk in cocoa and tea. She also makes soups and "I keep a stew pot going all the time as this is very economical". She says she is very well and happy. Mrs. D. of Birmingham appears to manage miraculously on 25/- housekeeping money of which 10/- goes in rent. She has only two children but even so her budget is magical. She was a cook before marriage which is a possible explanation. She says she has grapefruit, bacon and egg, bread and butter and marmalade for breakfast; meat, green vegetables and a boiled suet pudding for dinner and boiled cod twice a week. She says she never used tinned foods, "not even milk". She has good health.

The south, however, can also produce its good managers. Here is Mrs. E. of Sussex who pays 4/- rent out of 35/- housekeeping money and has six children all under 10. She is being supplied with milk by the Welfare Centre which she drinks in the middle of the morning and in the evening. She makes home-made cakes and jam, eats lots of vegetables out of her allotment and herrings and eggs when they are cheap. Onions, macaroni, cheese and suet pudding occur constantly in the diet. She says she worries about "knowing what to get for family to eat for cheapness and at same time most nutritious". She works very hard as she lives in an old-fashioned cottage and has to pump the water by hand but she makes no complaints about her health except backache.

There are bad managers too who do not do as much with their money as they might. The woman in Caerphilly who has only one child and whose budget is quoted later on eats very little eggs or fish and has altogether a poor diet. It is not surprising therefore to find that she suffers from bad turns of faintness and giddiness and palpitation, and gets very fagged with least exertion. Mrs. G. of Rochdale has two children, and pays 9/– rent out of housekeeping money of £1 10s. 0d. Her elder child is now 7 and suffered from rickets at two years of age and is still an out-patient. She eats a lot of tinned fruit and drinks a good deal of tea. She suffers from bad constipation for which she takes pills, and trembling and faintness. She has a good house with a bathroom and its own upstairs W.C. And again Mrs. H. of Essex, although she is poor, with five children and only 30/– a week housekeeping money does everything she can to avoid extra work. The consequence is that she eats tinned food and gives it to her children although there is, according to the Health Visitor, abundant fresh food to be obtained cheaply in the village. The visitor says "this woman is a great gossip and spends most of the day standing at the street door, the house is fairly clean and the children are clean but dependent on charity for most of their clothes which the mother is too idle to alter to fit." Mrs. F. of Liverpool is a widow and has four children under 8 to keep on total housekeeping money of £1 17s. 0d. She pays 10/6 rent. Her own diet is extremely poor consisting of bread and margarine, stew sometimes at dinner, no supper, and never eggs, fish or vegetables. She suffers from anæmia and she says it is due to worry and undernourishment but the Health Visitor says "the children look well fed and one cannot help believing that Mrs. F. is starving herself unnecessarily".

It is, however, not surprising to find that as soon as there is a little more money to spare it is spent on better food which the mother benefits by probably as quickly as the children. Mrs. D. of Croydon who has only two children and 52/– housekeeping money after the rent is paid, has an excellent diet in which Ovaltine, fresh fruit, Ryvita and cream cheese are frequent items. She obviously does not have to worry much about expenditure but in spite of this manages her time badly and says she has too much to do. She is one of the very few who pay for hired help. She says that she gets a woman in for one whole

day a week and gets help also with needlework. She adds:
"I cannot rest as I should with two children to look after
and most of the housework, and am constipated owing to
lack of daily exercise such as *brisk* walking and games".
She is on her feet "all day excepting for hurriedly eaten
meals", but in the evening she gets two-and-a-half hours'
leisure knitting, mending, playing games such as Lexicon,
Ping-pong, Tennis or Badminton ! She mentions she drinks
tea three times a day but "more in times of stress". And
in Newcastle the wife of a garage proprietor with only one
child has an excellent diet. She is one of the few people
who have coffee for breakfast; eggs and bacon, soup,
fresh meat, fish and fresh fruit occur in her menus.
She has £4 housekeeping money of which 17/6 goes in
rent.

Diet is only one factor influencing health but when a
woman is already in bad health proper food is an essential
agent in its cure. It is clear that many women realise this
but know that it is impossible to buy the right sort of food
for themselves. As has been pointed out in an earlier
chapter the diet must inevitably become worse when the
family moves to a more highly-rented house. A woman
in Rotherham realises this very clearly. She has just moved
to a Municipal Estate from a slum and she says "There is
now 3/- less to spend on food because my rent is 8/-
instead of 5/-". Her housekeeping money is 30/- after
the paying of the rent and she has six children. Her husband
is out of work. She suffers from headaches, dizziness,
constipation and indigestion and says that all of these
have been much worse lately. She writes "I simply cannot
feed and clothe properly husband and children on the
Means Test".

The main articles of diet are apparent in the accounts
that have been given above. Tea is on the whole not drunk
as often as might be expected and it is clear that the women
have learnt about this from the Welfare Centres. Most of

the mothers who attend Welfare Centres regularly say that they drink a good deal of water, and tea only with their meals. As exceptions to this a woman in Sheffield may be mentioned who buys 1½ lbs tea a week for herself and her husband and one small child ! A Paddington woman finds that "water lies heavy on the chest", so drinks tea. The Scots are greater tea drinkers apparently than the southerners and many of them say that they drink it five times a day and pretty strong. Other drinks are seldom mentioned. In some of the slums in Derby, which have been quoted above, mineral water and ginger beer are mentioned but this is probably because the women have been warned not to drink the water. Coffee is very seldom drunk and beer and spirits are hardly ever mentioned except with contempt.

It appears that nearly all milk is tinned, especially *in the country*. Fish is not at all a constant article of diet, is commoner in the north than in the south, and in the town than in the country. Fruit occurs quite often, sometimes even when funds are low but it is rarely other than oranges and bananas. Eggs are rarely used and when they are they are generally strictly limited to 1/– worth a week for the whole family. This may only buy six in the winter. Soups, salads and cheese are very rare. As a rule, supper is not eaten at all; if it is, it consists mostly of cocoa, (made with water and the addition of a little tinned milk), sometimes fish and chips and rarely bread and cheese. It must also be remembered that the quality of most of the articles of food bought is poor. This can be seen in the budgets given hereafter, e.g. a 2lb pot of marmalade for 8½d.; butter at 10d. a lb.; margarine at 4d. It is difficult to gauge actual quantities of food consumed by the mother, or indeed by any of the other members of the family. But in some instances the woman has given quantities for herself, and from these it seems that a tablespoonful of stew, and of vegetables, (even of potatoes) and two slices of bread and butter are the usual amounts of these foods eaten by her at the appropriate meal. That the quantity cannot ever be much larger than this is born out by the budgets and menus given at the end of this chapter. Even therefore in the few menus where there is apparently some variety, it is unlikely that the mother is getting a sufficient amount of food, and when as an aggravation of this shortage she eats her meals hurriedly and probably standing up, and without relish or appetite, it is made abundantly clear that in an undernourished family she is certainly the worst sufferer.

Much might be done with more education and better facilities but the basic difficulty of the great majority of these 1,250 mothers is the lack of financial resources. Until these are improved or food is very much cheaper it is quite clear that the mother above all cannot maintain the strength she needs for the laborious work and care of a growing family. It is not sufficient to give her a little extra milk in pregnancy only or while she is nursing, "It is customary to speak of nutrition in pregnancy as though it differed in some directions from nutrition at other periods of life . . . but the nutritional needs in pregnancy are those necessary to the continued efficiency of the function of nutrition throughout life . . . as well might we regard the taking of a steep hill as a feat additional to the normal function of a motor car as regard the making of a 7 lb baby as a feat additional to the normal function of a woman." (Sir Robert McCarrison at the British Medical Association Meeting in Belfast 1937).

BUDGETS AND MENUS

1. MRS. B. of Blackburn aged 23 has one child (Sheila) aged 3 and is pregnant. Her husband is unemployed, receives dole of 28/3 and her father lives with them. She speaks of chronic headache due, she thinks, to constipation.

She gives this account of her expenditure on food:—

Weekly List

2 lbs of Empire Butter = 10d. . . .	1	8
2 lbs of Sugar		4½
½ lb of Tea		9
1 Tin of Cocoa		5
12 lbs of Potatoes		8½
2 lbs of Carrots		1½
2 lbs of Onions		2½
½ lb of Bacon		5½
½ lb of Prunes for Sheila . . .		3
1 lb of Peas or Beans . . .		2½
2 lb jar of Marmalade . . .		8½
2 bars of Imp Soap . . .		5½
8 loaves = 3d.	2	0
Milk	1	0
	9	4

She then writes:—

"Meat for week I have to spend what I can spare after I have got the other things. I never buy any marjerine as one eat a bit of good butter and bread alone. What I have over from this I vary some weeks I get syrup or jam. Some times a few tomatoes nearly always I get a few apples for Sheila, then one week I need rice or sago as I make puddings three times a week, then I allow 2/6 for gas a week we have no gas stove it is only for lighting and we use two bags of coal a week my husband brings it as it is cheaper to do so it is 1/5 per bag. Some weeks I make a change and perhaps get fresh eggs instead of bacon or cheese than one week I have to buy metal polish and floor polish well I have to see what I can do without that week as I have only 11 shillings to spend on food.

"I have been getting extra three shillings per week from you but as I am expecting a baby shortly I have used this for Baby clothes as I had given what I had for Sheila, she is three years old. I thought perhaps this list might help you and I get my groceries in all at once except milk which I get each morning and meat also bread I get in two a day then I have not to use new bread but I pay for them all at once I have not got any special shop I go where I see it cheap and fresh. Now when I get Baby I am hoping that I can feed him myself as I have to buy a pram and a cot and they are so much better when they are fed than bottle fed I fed Sheila for seven months.

Perhaps this list may help someone as we get enough food

to last a week and although it is only plain we are not going
hungry or under fed we do not get any fancy stuff occasionally
I buy $\frac{1}{2}$ lb biscuits but I make a lot of soups and stews as these
are cheap and yet satisfy a man. I sometimes try and save
a few coppers each week until I have about 1/6 then I make the
following recipe

1 lb dried apricots	10*d.* or	1	0
3 lbs Sugar			6
	1 4 or	1	6

this makes 6 one pound jars of apricot jam so it is not dear.

"As regards clothes well my Husband usually gets work on
the Ribble in Summer so I have to get them then and take care
of them as I think that if you make yourself clean and tidy it is
one of the main things a darn or a patch is not a disgrace but
holes and dirt is. I have always tried to keep my home clean
although I have not a lot of furniture and Sheila always takes
and puts her coat and hat etc. in a drawer when she comes in
although she is only three. I bought her coat and hat at Marks
and Spencers at Blackpool last June and it cost 4/11 she wears
it every day and its just getting grubby looking now. Shoes are
an item that cost a lot but I try to get good ones for Sheila as
cheap ones are no use as they will not mend. I hope that you
will not be offended at this but I was thinking it would give you
an idea of how the unemployed man and his wife make their
money do. My man does not drink but he smokes and I do not
begrude them to him as drink would be far worse.

Yours respectfully,
(signed) B. B. . . ."

2. Mrs. V. lives in a slum street of small houses in Derby.
She is 40, and has three children, two girls and a boy;
her husband is a Railway Porter. Her housekeeping is
£1 19s. 0d., which she budgets for the week in the following
way:

Rent	.	.	.	11	0
2 bags coal	.	.	.	2	10
Death Insurance	.	.		9
Gas	.	.	.	1	0
4 lbs sugar	.	.	.		9
$\frac{1}{2}$ lb tea	.	.	.		9

3 boxes matches	.	.	.		3
Tin Milk	.	.	.		7½
1 lb rice	.	.	.		4
1 lb lard	.	.	.		4½
1 lb butter	.	.	.		9
Flour	.	.	.		7
Bacon	.	.	.		9
Eggs	.	.	.	1	0
Ambrosia	.	.	.		5
4 lbs potatoes	.	.	.		3
Butter beans	.	.	.		2
Cake	.	.	.		6
Fish for cooking	.	.	.		6
Bread	.	.	.	2	0
Meat	.	.	.	1	6
Potatoes, 8 lbs	.	.	.		6
Greens	.	.	.		3
Prunes	.	.	.		6
Custard powder	.	.	.		1½
Suet	.	.	.		2
Milk for week	.	.	.	1	6½
Papers	.	.	.		6
Soap	.	.	.		5
Wash powder	.	.	.		3½
Blue	.	.	.		1
Starch	.	.	.		1
Golden Syrup	.	.	.		9½
Cooking Apples	.	.	.		2
Suet	.	.	.		2
Bacon	.	.	.		9
Biscuits	.	.	.		6
Gas	.	.	.		3
Cheese	.	.	.		3
Cake	.	.	.		6
Cocoa	.	.	.		5½
Oxo	.	.	.		6
Stewing Meat	.	.	.		6
Peas	.	.	.		2
Box savings for stockings or Doctor	.			2	3½

£1 18 10

N.B. Potatoes are here given twice making 12 lbs. in all which is
a reasonable amount.

Her own diet for a week is given as:—

Saturday

Breakfast: 2 slices of toasts and dripping, 2 cups of tea
Dinner: Half of a small rice pudding and mug of lentil soup
Tea: 2 slices of bread and butter, 1 boiled egg, 2 cups of tea
Supper: 1 slice of bread and cheese, ½ pint pot of Ambrosia

Sunday

Breakfast:	2 slices of bread and poached egg, 2 cups of tea
Dinner:	Roast Beef, 2 spoonsful of butter beans, 2 spoonsful potatoes, boiled rubarb pudding, small helping
Tea:	2 cups of tea, 2 slices of brown and 1 white bread. 6 prunes with custard
Supper:	Bread and Butter (½ slice) ½ pint Ambrosia

Monday

Breakfast:	2 slices Bread and dripping, 2 cups of tea
Dinner:	Small piece of beef, 2 tablespoons of potatoes, piece of Yorkshire Pudding, 1 Baked Apple
Tea:	2 cups of tea, 3½ slices of bread and jam
Supper:	½ pint of Ambrosia

Tuesday

Breakfast:	2 cups of tea, 2½ slices bread and butter and golden syrup
Dinner:	Stewing meat, 2 spoons of mashed potatoes, cabbage 1 spoonful boiled suet pudding
Tea:	2 cups of tea, 2 slices bread and butter, boiled egg
Supper:	½ slice bread and cheese, ½ pint Ambrosia

Wednesday

Breakfast:	2 cupfull of tea, 2 slices bread and golden syrup, 1 banana
Dinner:	Boiled fish, 2 spoons mashed potatoes, cheese pudding
Tea:	Bread and butter, 2 slices, 2 pieces plain cake, 2 cups of tea
Supper:	½ pint Ambrosia, 3 biscuits

Thursday

Breakfast:	Toast and dripping, 2 slices, 2 cups of tea
Dinner:	Mashed potatoes 2 spoonsful cabbage 1 spoon boiled suet pudding with jam
Tea:	Bread and butter 2 slices, 1 boiled egg
Supper:	½ pint Ambrosia 3 biscuits

Friday

Breakfast:	3 slices of bread and butter 2 cups of tea
Dinner:	Piece of fish baked, mashed potatoes 2 spoonfuls, 4 tablespoonfull of rice pudding.
Tea:	Bread and butter 3 slices 1 piece of cake 2 cups of tea
Supper:	½ pint pot of Ambrosia

The house is very bad. It has no bath, the boiler is broken and the Landlord refuses to mend it: there were bad floods in 1932, and several feet of water in the house, since when it has always been damp; the W.C. is 25 yards from the house; there is a rag and bone shop in the yard next door, and this gives out unpleasant smells; the house is hemmed in by factories. Mrs. V. says she was quite well till seven months ago, when her husband had a serious illness. She was then six months pregnant, but in order to eke out the income she went out to work a little, and had to nurse her husband in the house which made the work very hard. Since then she has been feeling very ill, and has great difficulty in nursing the baby who is now four months old. The Health Visitor says she is a sensible woman, and the husband is very good to her, and being himself a trained ambulance man, he is very useful in illness.

3. Mrs. C. of Rotherham is 37 living in a Municipal Housing Estate. She has eight children and her husband is a labourer but has been unemployed for two years. Her housekeeping money is £2 5s. 0d. out of which she pays 7/10 rent, she gives her diet as under:—

Breakfast: Tea, dont usually eat any breakfast
Dinner: Bread and lard or margerine; dinner, occasionally which includes stew meat and potatoes. By time you have served 9 of them you have had yours
Tea: Consists of tea, bread and butter, tinned tomatoes and black pudding
Supper: 3d. of chips and 1d. fish for five or six of us about 3 times a week

Mrs. C. suffers from headache, rheumatism and tuberculosis, due she thinks to the bad housing conditions in which she was living till recently. She says her main difficulties are "money matters owing to large family to keep also owing to my health have occasionaly to go in San and have girl of 15 and Mrs. Ward to do washing. Baking and Housework and Riddiculous gas fire you burn money an still no rooms get heated or dried only 1 sq. yard of your floor only living room to Dry clothes in and Back Kitchen so small. Children unable to attend school having no boots and unable to get any Teachers always sending and grumbling".

She has had extra milk from the Clinic during three months only of her pregnancy, (her youngest child is seven months) and a grant of food at her confinement, and she has, since the birth of the last baby been given Birth Control advice at the Municipal Clinic. Milk and Parrish's food are allowed to the older children throughout the year. Mrs. C. used to have an allowance of extra food from the T.B. dispensary but that has now stopped and as a consequence she never now eats eggs.

4. Mrs. D. of Derby is 35 years old and has five children (all boys) and lives in a small Corporation house. Her husband is an unemployed labourer and her housekeeping is £2 1s. 0d. of which she gives the following particulars of expenditure:—

Rent	12	6
Gas and Electric Light (6d. each)	1	0
Clothing Club	3	0
Boot Club	1	0
Coal, 2 cwt.	3	0
Milk	2	9½
Bread	3	3½
Insurance	1	6
2 lbs margerine @ 4d.		8
½ lb butter @ 1/–		6
6 lbs sugar	1	3
½ lb tea		9
¼ lb cocoa		4
¼ lb lard		3
½ lb cheese		3
1 doz. eggs	1	6
1 lb bacon		11
1 bag self-raising flour		5
1 lb loose peas		4
2 boxes matches		2
1 lb soap		5
1 Packet wash powder		2
1 Packet starch		1
1 lb Soda		1
1 Packet Salt		1
¼ lb Cooked ham @ 1/10		5½
Old Potatoes		6
1 lb New Potatoes		3
1 lb Onions		2
Radishes, spring onions and lettuce		6

Cauliflower	.	.	.	.		2
Oranges .	.	.	.	.		3
Piece of Meat (beef) @ 1/3	.	.		1	3
Breast of mutton @ 8d.	.	.	.		4
½ lb Corn Beef .	.	.	.		3
Piece of Codfish	.	.	.		5½
Sweets for Kiddies	.	.	.		2

$$£2 \quad 1 \quad 0$$

Mrs. D. also gives her complete weekly diet:—

Sunday
Breakfast: 2 slices of bread, two pieces of bacon, two cups of tea
Dinner: ½ pint water, 3 potatoes, two tablespoonfuls of peas, small bit of beef, small portion of rice pudding
Tea: 2 slices of bread and butter, an egg, two cups of tea, piece of cake
Supper: 1 Cup of cocoa

Monday
Breakfast: 2 cups of tea, 1 slice of toast and butter
Dinner: 2 tablespoonfuls of potatoes, stewed meat and gravy, ½ pint of water
Tea: 2 slices of bread and butter and jam, 2 cups of tea, 1 piece of cake
Supper: 1 cup of cocoa

Tuesday
Breakfast: 2 cups of tea and 2 slices of brown bread and butter
Dinner: 3 potatoes, 1 tablespoonful of cauliflower and stewed mutton, stewed rhubarb and custard
Tea: 2 slices of bread and butter and radishes, 1 piece of cake and 2 cups of tea
Supper: 1 cup of cocoa and a slice of bread and dripping

Wednesday
Breakfast: Two cups of tea, slice and a half of bread and dripping
Dinner: 3 new potatoes, 2 tablespoonsful of peas and sausage, ½ pint of water
Tea: 2 cups of tea, 2 slices of bread and butter, one tomato and one piece of cake
Supper: 1 cup of cocoa and slice of bread and dripping

Thursday
Breakfast: 2 cups of tea, slice of bacon and slice of bread
Dinner: 1 new laid egg and chipped potatoes, 1 slice of bread, ½ pint of water, 1 cup of cocoa at 11 o'clock
Tea: 2 cups of tea, 2 slices of bread and butter and lettuce, and 2 small cakes, 1 orange at 3 o'clock
Supper: 1 cup of cocoa

Friday

Breakfast:	2 cups of tea, 1½ slices bread and butter and jam
Dinner:	2 slices of bread, 1 slice of bacon, 2 tablespoonsful of tomatoes and ½ pint water
Tea:	2 slices of bread and butter and 1 boiled egg, two cups of tea
Supper:	1 cup of cocoa

Saturday

Breakfast:	2 cups of tea, 1 slice of bread and jam
Dinner:	2 slices of bread and corn beef, ½ pint of water
Tea:	2 slices of bread and butter and radishes and onions, 2 cups of tea
Supper:	1 cup of cocoa

It should be particularly noticed here that there is only 2 lbs of margarine and ½ lb of butter a week for 2 adults and 4 children (aged from 9–4;—there is also a baby of 3 months whom Mrs. D. is nursing.) There are only 1 doz. eggs, and yet she says she eats 3 a week herself; and only 3d. worth of oranges,—the only fruit.

5. Mrs. C. lives in a "nicely situated villa" in a "nice quiet spot" in Caerphilly. She has one child and her husband is a collier. Her housekeeping is £2 10s. 0d. from a full working week but she says her husband is delicate so she sometimes only gets 30/–. She is 29 years old.

Below is her average of living per week, "when times are good":—

	s.	d.
Rent	10	0
Light	2	0
Coal	2	0
Firewood		6
Clothing Club	1	6
Boot Club	1	6
Insurance	1	0
Milk	1	6
Meat	3	6
Groceries (on the average)	18	6
Bread	3	0
Fish	1	6
Vegetables	1	3
Sunday meat (about)	2	6
	£2 10	3

Breakfast:	Bread and butter for all, but porridge for change
Dinner:	Fresh Veg. when possible to get with potatoes and little meat, sometimes suet pudding
Tea:	Bread and butter and cake when possible with little jam
Supper:	Very little supper. Very little tinned food used

Compare this budget with that of Mrs. D. of Derby above.

6. Mrs. T. lives in three rooms on the first floor of a tenement house in Arbroath; 25 people use the W.C. She is 32 and has five children, a boy of 7 and four girls of 14, 8, 3 years and a baby of 14 months. Her husband is unemployed and she cleans offices every morning, her total housekeeping is 36/9. Her chief trouble is lack of water laid on to her rooms, it has to be carried from the washing house. She suffers from headaches.

Out of the 36/9 housekeeping the regular weekly payments are:—

			s.	d.
Rent	.	.	5	6
Coal	.	.	3	4
Gas .	.	.	3	0
			11	10

so that there is 24/11 left for food and clothing for the family of seven.

Mrs. T. gives the following family menus:—

Breakfast:	Porridge, Tea, rolls
Dinner:	Soup (Broth, potato, lentil, etc.) Potatoes
Tea:	Bread and butter, an egg if cheap
Supper:	Tea or cocoa, bread and butter, jam

The Health Visitor says the house is "very clean and tidy". The husband was in hospital for two years as the result of a neglected accident when on farm work and he has now lost a leg due to this accident. The income is derived from parish relief 20/–, half of her husband's insurance 8/9, (he keeps the other half), and her own wage for cleaning offices 8/–.

When the second and third child were born, (now aged 8 and 7) Mrs. T. was in bed three days for her confinement. The district nurse attended her. For the youngest child she was in bed for ten days. Since then she has been much troubled with a festering breast.

7. Mrs. N. lives in tiny rooms in squalid surroundings in Derby. She suffers from kidney trouble, backache, constipation, headache and tonsilitis periodically.

She gives her weekly diet as:—

Breakfast:	2 cups of weak tea
Dinner:	Half of 2d. worth of fried smelt, 1 slice of bread, 1 cup of tea
Tea:	2 pieces of bread and butter, Radishes, 2 cups of tea
Supper:	Roast potatoes and salt

She also says "More food is available on Friday when unemployment insurance money comes. There is then fried fish for supper".

Her income is 29/3, which is spent as follows:—

	s.	d.
Rent	4	6
Arrears of rent		6
Clothing Club	3	0
Weekly payment for pram . .	1	0
Insurance	1	6
2 cwt. of coal	3	0
School dinners for two children . .		10
Baby's food from Clinic . . .		8
	15	0

leaving 14/3 for food for herself, husband and three children, aged 5, 3, and 5 months, and for all household utensils.

8. Mrs. A. of Derby is 25 years old and has four children, a girl of 6 years, three boys of 4, 3, and 1, and is pregnant. She lives in a four-roomed cottage in a slum court which is due to be demolished in slum-clearance scheme. There

is no gas or copper, only oil lamps for light and the water has to be fetched from 40 yards away in the yard. There is no W.C. only a tub lavatory which the family have to share with others. Her husband is an unemployed labourer and the total income is 35/-. This is divided into the following regular payments:—

					s.	d.
Rent	.	.	.	.	5	0
Clothing Club	.	.	.		2	0
Pot Club	.	.	.		1	0
Coal	.	.	.		2	8
Pram and Furniture	.	.		1	6
Insurance	.	.	.		1	0
Tobacco for husband	.	.		1	0
					14	2

leaving £1/0/10 for food, cleaning materials, and extras.

Mrs. A's. own meals are given as:—

Breakfast: Cup of tea, porridge and milk, 1 slice of bread and butter
Dinner: New potatoes and bacon, cup of tea
Tea: Boiled egg, 2 slices of bread and butter, 2 cups of tea, orange
Supper: Bread and cheese, 1 cup of cocoa, 2 spoonfuls of condensed milk

9. Mrs. R. of Rochdale who is 24 lives in two rooms of a back-to-back house; part of the street is condemned; she has one child of 2 years and her husband is unemployed. Her housekeeping is £1 8s. 0d. which she budgets as under:—

					s.	d.
Rent	.	.	.	.	6	7
Clothing Club	.	.	.		1	0
Insurance	.	.	.		1	6
Coal	.	.	.		2	11
Furniture	.	.	.		5	0
Gas	.	.	.		1	9
					18	9

which leaves 9/3 to feed the family of three, and to buy cleaning utensils.

The mother gives the following as her average weekly meals:—

Breakfast: Bread and butter, cocoa
Dinner: Bread, vegetables, gravy (oxo or bone gravy) and milk pudding
Tea: Bread and jam, or an apple, or orange, tea
Supper: Cup of cocoa

She also says she has an egg twice a week and fresh fish once a week.

Mrs. R. suffers from valvular heart disease due to scarlet fever, anæmia and gastritis. She has attended the Tuberculosis dispensary, so that although she does not mention tubercle amongst the ailments, it seems clear that she is suffering, or has suffered from it.

10. Mrs. T. lives in a self-contained flat in Chelsea, consisting of three rooms and a scullery. She is 29 and has four children and is six months pregnant. Her husband is a cellarman, and gives her 37/6 a week out of which she pays the rent.

Housekeeping money 37/6 detailed as to regular payments as follows:—

					s.	d.
Rent	.	.	.	.	10	6
Club doctor	.	.	.	.	1	1
Insurance	.	.	.	.	1	8
Coal (paid all the year round) .	.	2	0
Gas about .	.	.	.	2	4
Clothing	.	.	.	.	2	0
					19	7

leaving 17/11, or just under 3/– a head, for food and cleaning.

She has not felt well ever since the first confinement, four-and-a-half years ago. She had severe post-partum hæmorrhage after every confinement, for which her Club doctor gives occasional tonics, and she gets advice from the Ante-natal Clinic. At present she rests as much as she can because of her pregnancy, but usually she is 15 hours a day on her feet, and her "leisure" is spent in taking the children out. She says she has no money for bus-rides or pictures. She spends 6d. a week for the whole family on fruit; only buys eggs when they are 1d. each, and twice a week she has cabbage or tomatoes. She is extremely anæmic. She was a cook before marriage.

11. Mrs. H. R. of Fulham has two children, a boy of 2 years and a girl aged 6. The family live in three rooms and a scullery in a "decent" street but the rooms are small and damp with a lot of steam from cooking. The husband is a lorry driver and had a bad accident a year ago and has not worked since; he still attends hospital three times a week. The question of compensation is not yet settled and meantime Mrs. H. R. has a total income of £2 14s. 0d. a week. She herself suffers from bad headaches due to worry and being blind in one eye, (she was advised by the Eye Hospital three years ago to have glasses but cannot afford them), depression and neuritis; she is 31 years old.

The family budget is given as follows:—

					s.	d.
Rent	.	.	.	.	18	0
Furniture payments		.	.	.	3	0
Insurance	.	.	.	.	1	10
Electric Light		.	.	.	1	0
Gas	.	.	.	.	2	6
Coal	.	.	.	.	2	0
Clothing Club		.	.	.	1	6
Milkman	.	.	.	.	2	3½

Regular payments   £1 12 1½

leaving £1/1/10½ per week for food, utensils, cleaning, etc.

The family menus are detailed as:—

Breakfast: Quaker oats, Nevilles White Bread, Stork margarine, shop marmalade or jam (a 2lb jar serves the family for a week) and occasionally home-made jam, tea. ½ pint of milk does for everyone's breakfast including the children's drink

Dinner: Breast of lamb (or ribs, barley, oxo),
Stewing beef for pie, lasts two days
Fillet of fish
Tin of Libby's Milk 3d. (this is found to be cheaper than custard powder)
Not pudding every day but occasionally dumplings, jam roll, etc.

Tea: Bread, margarine, jam, piece home-made cake sometimes, tea

Supper: Cup of Camp Coffee, fried fish sometimes, dripping toast sometimes, but usually only bread

The mother drinks tea four times a day.

12. Mrs. F. lives in an old three-roomed cottage in Essex, is 40 years old, married to an Army Pensioner, and has three children, a boy of 4 years and two girls of 4 and 2½. She gives her menus as under:—

Breakfast: Bread and margarine, tea with tinned milk

Dinner: One 3 lb. joint per week, 1 rabbit, breast of mutton about 3 lbs. (for whole family), potatoes and vegetables and suet pudding

Tea: Bread and dripping or margarine

Supper: Bread and dripping with onion and cocoa with milk

The Health Visitor writes, "The husband of this woman gets a whole time disability pension, through War Service, of 28/- per week. Out of that there is rent 5/- per week, coal 3/2, doctor's bills, etc. I believe in this case the woman's ill health is through lack of better food, and worry." She drinks tea only at breakfast and tea. She says she generally feels fit and well, but suffers from constant headaches, due she thinks to the want of more substantial food, and flatulence due to the same cause. She received a pint of milk a day from the Welfare Centre for one year.

13. Mrs. B. has five children, three boys of 14, 8 and 2 years and two girls of 12 and 11 years. She lives in a four-roomed old cottage in Rotherham and her husband is a greengrocer, her average money for housekeeping is 30/-, out of which she pays 8/2 in rent.

She gives her weekly diet for the family as:—

Breakfast:	Cup of tea, bacon and bread
Dinner:	Joint and vegetables three times, other days eggs and tomatoes
Tea:	Cup of tea, cheese, boiled mutton, or fish, kippers
Supper:	Fish and chips, bacon. Tinned food:—salmon, or fruit occasionally

Mrs. B. also says, "My husband is a greengrocer and works partly on his own account and I never know from one week to another how much I shall have to carry on with and I have 5 children".

She makes no complaints about her health and says she feels perfectly well.

14. Mrs. G. aged 24, lives in a house on a new building estate in Durham. She is married to a miner and has two children, a boy of 4½ and a girl aged 2. Her housekeeping money, after paying the rent, is 36/-. Her diet is given as:—

Breakfast:	*Choice of:*—Tea, cocoa and coffee, bread (brown and white) jam, banana, marmalade, lemon curd, occasional egg and porridge
Dinner:	*Choice of:*—Beef, occasionally pork, fish, milk puddings, soups, Yorkshire puddings, boiled suet puddings, liver, bacon, pease puddings, green vegetables
Tea:	*Choice of:*—Tea, brown and white bread, cheese, kippers, fresh herrings, jam, scones, teacakes, fresh fruit, occasionally cake
Supper:	*Choice of:*—Tea, fried fish, fresh fruit pie, brown bread and butter, green salads, cheese, meat pastes, tomatoes

Mrs. G. says she does not use tinned foods except an occasional tin of fruit and milk. She has fresh fish three or four times weekly but fresh vegetables at the week-ends only.

Her leisure consists of half-a-day weekly when she attends the bowling club of which she is a member, or sits in the local Welfare grounds. She also goes out regularly every day for one hour. She has learnt about health from the local Welfare Centre, and from the Press.

She feels well except for debility following pneumonia, and for this she occasionally takes fresh milk. She gets 1/– worth of eggs a week for the family.

15. Mrs. B. lives in two rooms in a house over a shop in Bermondsey. She is 39, has had eight children of whom six are living, their ages ranging from 12 to 2 years; her husband is a carman and gives her £2 4s. 0d. for house-keeping.

She says her weekly meals consist of:—

Breakfast:	Bread and margarine, tea
Dinner:	"Daily Sketch" or Bread and Cornbeef
Tea:	Bread and margarine
Supper:	Cannot afford them

When asked if she drinks much tea between these meals she said "Two cups because I cannot afford any more because I have 8 of us to keep and only husband at work". They live in what she calls a respectable neighbourhood and pay 7/6 rent. In answer to the question whether her day's work is too hard for her she says firmly "No, it is not". She doesn't feel well, and suffers from faintness and headaches, because she is "sun-starved." She takes castor oil and lemon for this, and says she cannot afford doctors.

16. Mrs. F. living in one room in a poor district in East London is 42 and has no children. Her husband is un-employed and she goes out charring daily; her house-keeping money is 12/– which is what she earns herself.

Her menus are:—

Breakfast:	Bread, butter, tea
Dinner:	
Monday :	Cornbeef
Tuesday :	Fried Fish
Wednesday :	Stew
Thursday :	1 egg and chips
Friday :	Fish
Saturday :	Meat Pudding
Sunday :	Potatoes (chop)

Tea:	Bread, butter, tea
Supper:	Tea

She says that her husband does "not receive dole or P.A.C. so find it difficult to keep him clean as I would like to".

CHAPTER VIII

CONCLUSIONS AND RECOMMENDATIONS

IT seems clear that there are three inter-connected factors which cause the life of the working-class housewife to be too difficult and strenuous. The first is poverty, the second ill-health and the third lack of trained knowledge.

I. *Poverty*

All, except a very few of the families of whom these 1,250 women are the mothers and managers are too poor. Nearly all are too poor to buy the healthy satisfaction even of their primary needs, food, fuel and light, decent housing and a minimum of clothing and household equipment. Very few are able even to dream of a cultural and social standard which, as a minimum, should include a little comfort and pleasure, some travel, the luxury of helping a friend, books, newspapers, subscriptions to churches, clubs and political organisations—toys and sweets for the children.

Nearly all assessments of the minimum needs of the working man and his family are concerned with the commodities without which he would cease to live, for he would die either of starvation or cold, or of both; with less than a certain amount of these commodities he suffers in health and physical efficiency. These estimates of "basic needs" almost completely omit the demands of the spirit[1]; but

[1] Mr. Rowntree's minimum of 53/- for a town worker and a family of three children allows 9/- a week for "personal sundries"; of this 4/1 is allocated to Unemployment and Health Insurance, contributions to sick clubs and Trade Unions etc., and travelling to and from work; leaving 4/11 for everything else in the way of newspapers, beer, tobacco, presents, holidays, books and travelling etc.

that these insist upon some degree of satisfaction, often at the cost of the "sops of the body" is proved by the amount which is in fact spent on "luxuries" even by the poorest. In any family enough must be found somehow for the expenses which inevitably arise at some time—in some families at all times—fares to and from work, or in search of work, writing letters, medical and nursing fees. And over and above this, there *must* be something for newspapers, entertainment and personal indulgence. It is fantastic therefore to suppose that every half-penny is or should be spent on what are called primary necessities. Moreover, even if it were, very few housewives have the opportunity or knowledge to spend with that degree of prudence and economy which would insure full value to their money. So that it is obvious that most of these families, who are a sample of a very large section of the community, cannot obtain the basic needs of a spiritually and physically healthy life.

In a household in which deficiency plays a far larger part than fulfilment, it is certain that the mother, who is the chancellor of the family exchequer, will deprive herself, instinctively or deliberately, for the sake of her husband and children. The strength and persistence of this maternal feeling must be reckoned with, and any service or reform which aims at the increase of the mother's welfare must either be capable of conducing directly, *in her judgment*, to the benefit of her family, or must be administered in such a way that she cannot divert it away from herself and use it for her children alone.

Economic assistance should be given in the following ways:—(a) *Increase of wages*. It is beyond the scope of this book to discuss any of the more fundamental proposals for the reduction of poverty, but it is necessary to point out that a very large section of the population fall below the income level which has been indicated as a minimum on which people can maintain a healthy living. It is, therefore, appropriate to urge the extension of existing machinery, such as Trade Board Acts and Trades Union organisation to those industries where wages are still too low to allow for the decencies or even the necessities of life. This would at least result in an increase of wages to the extent that the productivity and, in some cases, the better organisation of the industry would permit.

(b) *Increased communal provision for children.* A low wage brings the worst evils in families where there are dependent children, and especially where there are many dependent children. Mr. Rowntree's minimum (53/– for the town worker, or, at prices ruling to-day, 55/6) allows only for a family of three children. He estimates, however, that 42% of all children belong to families in which there are four or more dependent children, i.e. children under 14 years old, and that 34·5% are in that position for five or more years. No exact estimate has yet been made of the total numbers of workers receiving less than Mr. Rowntree's minimum, but it is probable that 40% of all urban workers, and nearly all agricultural labourers are in this position. Sir John Orr estimates that about 25% of all children under 14 are now in families with an income of less than 10/– per head per week, (i.e. considerably less than Mr. Rowntree's minimum). It is clear, therefore, that even were this very modest minimum attained, which is far from being the case at present, a high proportion of children, and, *a fortiori*, their mothers, would still for a considerable period of their lives suffer from a deficiency of some of the basic necessities of life.

It is clear that quite apart from her own physical privation, the mother of such families has an intolerable burden to bear. She is faced not only with the lack of sufficient income to buy for her family what is needed, but with the constant strain of uneasiness caused by the shadow of unemployment, with the fear of a reduction in an already insufficient wage, and with the fear of running into debt while endeavouring to meet such unvarying obligations as rent, hire-purchase, insurance, etc.

The larger the family, the greater the difficulties and responsibilities, and the smaller relatively are the resources and strength with which to meet them. The first and most pressing need therefore is to break this very vicious circle by insuring that the existence of the children should not make the family poorer or the mother progressively less able to meet her increasing responsibilities. The national as well as the individual aspect of the falling birth-rate, which, if the present tendency continues, will lead to a drastic reduction in the population, should be borne in mind in this connection.

The methods which can be adopted by the community to provide help in bringing up a family are (i) an extension of the social services for children and (ii) the establishment of a system of cash payments, as family allowances.

(i) *The Extension of the Social Services.* Although there has been of late years a considerable extension of the social services as they affect children, there are many directions in which a further development is urgently necessary. These vary from an increase of the schemes for the provision of free and cheap milk for children, both in school and under school age, to a considerable increase in the number of nursery schools and day nurseries. Moreover it is highly desirable that the educational system of this country should be developed in such a way that each child should have provided for him by the community the education best suited for his abilities and his needs, instead of such provision being, as at present, largely dependent on the income of his parents.

(ii) *Family Allowances.* Young children are no longer an economic asset, as they were until about the last quarter of last century. Even assuming that the child begins to earn at 14 or 15, and that the family is slightly better off with such wages as a child of that age can command, there is a minimum period of 14 years during which the parents have to maintain the child, and to maintain him at a compulsorily higher standard than was considered necessary fifty or even twenty years ago. Undoubtedly the age at which a child is allowed to earn will be raised still further, and the laws regulating the care and health of the dependent child, far from lessening the responsibilities of the parents, will continue to increase their obligations, financial and otherwise.

In recent social legislation there has been a welcome recognition of the *principle*, that if the family income is to be commensurate with its needs, it must increase with the size of the family. Income tax allowances for dependent children, scales of assistance adopted by the Unemployment Insurance Acts, rent rebate schemes, grants made to the parents of secondary-school children, are all instances of the acknowledgment of this doctrine. The Unemployment Statutory Committee has itself drawn attention to the conflict of principle in a system under which a man who is out of work receives an income in proportion to the size of his family, while one who is in work does not; both the Unemployment Statutory Committee and the Unemployment Assistance Board are thereby placed in a difficult position, for the establishment of scales of assistance which it considers necessary for the minimum support of children, would, unless modified, exceed, in the case of lower paid workers with several children, the normal wage of the father when in work.

It is both undesirable and impracticable for wages themselves to vary according to the needs of the individual worker. Therefore, in order that adequate provision for children may be guaranteed, the Woman's Health Enquiry Committee strongly urge that some scheme of Family Allowances, independent of and in addition to wages, should be provided by the community on behalf of each child, and made payable to the mother. In this way, not only would the anomalies as between employed and unemployed wage-earners vanish, but the working-mothers themselves would take their place in the economic system. They control the family expenditure and perform the various tasks in connection with the care of the family. It is right, therefore, that they should be entitled, as they were under the system of separation allowances during the last war, to an income proportionate to the number of mouths they have to feed, instead of being as at present entirely dependent on the earning capacity and the generosity of their husbands, or on the chance of his finding work at all.

The extension of the social services cannot go all the way. Rent (except where rent rebates are provided in municipal houses), the needs of the pre-school child, or the individual needs of a delicate child, the hundred and one small services which are required for children in the home, are and must remain dependent on the money that the mother has to spend. Power should be given to her to determine in some measure for herself, the needs of herself and her children, more than is possible if the help granted by the community is entirely in kind. For example, it would be better, instead of having a system of free school dinners, to have dinners provided at school for payment, in order that the mother may decide whether it is better for the child to be fed at home or at school; similarly, although there should be the provision of facilities for the performance of certain household tasks in a communal centre, the housewife should be free to choose whether to do these jobs herself, at home or at the centre, or to pay someone else to do them.

The way in which such a scheme should be financed, the question whether the whole sum should be raised by taxation, or whether it should form part of the social insurance system of the country, the question of the amount of the allowances, and whether they should be provided for all children, or should start with the second or third in the family, need not be discussed here. Suffice it to say that many Family Allowance schemes are being put forward, the estimated cost of which varies from ten million to a hundred million pounds, and the administration of which would vary from a national scheme raised by taxation or through social insurance to schemes financed by industrial or professional pools. Family Allowance schemes have been established by law in many countries in Europe and in the Dominions. Of these it is interesting to note that where strong Labour movements exist as in France and Belgium, Australia and New Zealand, the system has the whole-hearted support of Labour.

(c) *Housing*. The provision of a sufficient number of decent houses at rents which the workers can pay, remains a matter of extreme urgency. Ever since the War it has been recognised that private enterprise could not, without help from the State, make good the appalling deficiency of decent working-class homes, especially for the larger and poorer families who can only afford a very low and uneconomic rent. Six successive governments have passed as many Housing Acts, but in spite of remarkable achievement,[1] there has been appalling waste of money[2] and, what is worse, there is still, on the standard of one decent house per family at a rent which can be paid, a very serious deficiency.[3]

---

[1] Over three and a half million houses have been built since the War, in England and Wales.

[2] Under the Addison Act, (1919) 176,000 subsidized houses were built at a cost for 40 years of £8,000,000 per annum—£1 per week per house.

[3] The increase of separate families from 1921–31 (Census years) in England and Wales was 1,494,000. The increase of structurally separate dwellings in the same period was 1,373,000. Therefore the shortage of houses which in 1921 was estimated at 710,000 had *increased* by 1931 to 831,000. Mr. C. J. Hill of the Economic Intelligence Department has estimated that the 1941 Census will show a further increase of separate families of 668,000; and that in 1951 there will be a further increase of 146,000. It will be seen therefore that to have made up the deficiency by 1941 a net increase of 1½ million houses (over 1931) will be necessary. Actually since 1931 up to the present, about 2 million houses, *of all sorts*, have been built; but less than ½ million of these are subsidized working-class houses, (i.e. capable of being let at low rents). Moreover, nearly ¼ million houses, *practically all working-class* have been closed or demolished, and a great many more are scheduled for early clearance. It is highly probable that the shortage will not have been overtaken by 1941 even if the process of "filtering-up", (i.e. people who can afford to do so vacating the lower-

The main principles which the Women's Health Enquiry Committee wish to formulate are:—

First, that every family must have as soon as possible a good dwelling which shall be large enough for its requirements, and cheap enough to insure that the rent is not paid at the cost of any of the other basic necessities of good health. For this purpose, subsidies should be attached to the particular families who are in need of them and for as long as they are in such need. Rent rebates, which are a practical way of allocating subsidies, should be on a sliding scale based on the two factors of family income and the size of family. The administration of such a scheme can only be in the hands of Local Authorities, on whom therefore an obligation should be placed to provide a sufficiency of low-rented houses for the poorer families.

Secondly, when this quantitative problem is solved, the question of higher standards of housing should be considered. It is obviously useless to legislate against slums or over-crowding until there is sufficient alternative accommodation. Then it is to be hoped that the standard of over-crowding will be raised so that not only are the minimum requirements of hygiene and good health satisfied, but a certain degree of real privacy is possible for the individual members of the family.[1] It must be borne in

---

rented houses and moving into unsubsidized higher-rented houses) were steady and complete, which is far from being the case; and that therefore the shortage is likely still to be acute in the direction where houses are most urgently needed, low-rented working-class.

It has been estimated that another 2 million houses will be required by 1951, and that when these are built a further million will be needed to satisfy the higher standard which will be demanded as soon as the quantity deficiency is made good.

[1] Over-crowding is fully defined in the 1936 Housing Act, Part IV, Section 58, and the Fifth Schedule. Roughly speaking two persons per room are allowed provided that unless they are living together as husband and wife, they are, if over the age of 10, of the same sex. "Room" means any room in the house or flat not less than 50 sq. feet; and in order that two persons should sleep in one room, that room must be at least 110 sq. feet, i.e. 10 by 11 feet. It will be recognised that this is not a high standard.

mind, however, that the enforcement of over-crowding regulations may have the effect of restricting the number of children in a family to a degree that would be disastrous to the nation; and that therefore there must be a large number of available houses really big enough for a numerous family, who being as a rule the poorer family will not be able to pay as much per square foot of space as the small family in the small house; in other words the larger house will cost more per cubic foot to the Housing Authority, than the smaller one. This must not be allowed to be a deterrent to building such houses. If responsible people are to be encouraged to bring up as large a family as their health and strength and inclination allow, they should be offered as high a standard of comfort and pleasantness in their homes as is attainable by the smaller family. Mr. Carr-Saunders has pointed out the deleterious effects on all population problems of the stereotyped small house, which has been the standard pattern since the War.

Thirdly, it is immediately practicable to "convert" a large number of existing dwellings into comfortable and healthy homes for small families, at far less cost than is required for the building of new houses. Local Authorities should exercise to a far greater extent than they now do their powers of compulsory purchase. The vested interests of speculative builders and property owners (often the same persons), are often a severe obstruction to progress in housing, and must be dealt with, if necessary, by drastic measures, such as the taxation of land values. The conversion of the large old-fashioned house has been shown by the Public Utility Companies to give an economic return; and if this work were undertaken by bodies whose primary concern is not profit, but the benefit of the tenants, the monetary contribution made by the community, in the form of housing subsidies would be freed for the primary need of homes for the larger and poorer families.

Fourthly, schemes should immediately be put into effect to ameliorate the condition of rural housing, particularly from the point of view of the housewife's work. The present difficulties of water, lighting and heating should no longer be tolerated, even for old cottages. When these are remedied, one of the causes of rural depopulation will disappear.

In general it is to be hoped that all Housing Authorities will invite the views of women and make use of their services in architecture, house-management and sanitary inspection, to a much larger extent than is done at present. Healthy surroundings for children are comparatively easily visualised and planned by men as well as by women. But the thousand and one details which contribute to the health and efficiency of the housewife constitute a problem which can only be solved by the imagination and grasp of detail which a woman is capable of bringing to the task. Outside as well as inside the house, her comfort must be considered. Important as play-grounds are for the children, they at least have the relief of air and space at school. The mother needs a pleasant garden at her door, which will give her not only agreeable recreation and rest, but a cheerful outlook in her hours of solitary work.

The provision of healthy and lovely homes is for the benefit of every member of the family; but for the mother it would mean an even greater increase of spiritual and physical well-being than for her husband and children. Air, light, space and pleasantness will alter the colour of every hour of her life, and, while lightening her labour, will bring it the reward to which every housewife is entitled, pride and comfort in her home.

II. *Ill-Health*

The physical condition of most working-class mothers is no doubt due primarily to poverty, but, as this enquiry has indicated, poverty is only one of the influences which lead to the deplorably low standard of fitness and vitality.

The working-woman will always be more liable to minor sickness than the man, partly because of the strain of maternity, but mostly because even when her financial condition is improved, her waking hours will be full of a multitude of small but pressing activities which will make it less easy for her to *protect* her health against the results of over-fatigue, lack of fresh air and exercise, irregularity of feeding, etc., etc.

(a) *Medical Services*. The attitude to health of such women is apt to be a combination of courage, prudery and ignorance. There is urgently needed some form of medical service which is easily accessible at all times, both in sickness and in health, which will help them to form a high standard of physical well-being and to maintain it, and which will dispel the shyness they are apt to feel at present either on grounds of prudery or for fear of making a fuss about nothing. Owing to the fact that the National Health Insurance system makes no provision for the wife of an insured man, she has still to call in a private doctor when she feels ill. This leaves the decision to the woman herself, who will naturally postpone this step as long as possible. The greater her ignorance and her fortitude, and the lower her standard and her financial resources, the longer will she defer seeking the advice she needs. The experience of the maternity and child welfare services has shown that centres where the woman is encouraged to pay regular visits, and where she can have friendly talks, even when she is not ill, with medical experts or nurses, have a value far beyond the occasional visits to a private practitioner. Their function is in the first place preventive as well as curative; they teach the mother a great deal both directly and indirectly on matters of hygiene and diet; they give her opportunities for meeting others and learning also from them; and above all they diffuse an atmosphere of friendliness and confidence which is an invaluable asset in building and maintaining the intricate structure of a woman's health.

At present such Clinics exist for the expectant and nursing mother and her small children. They need, however, to be increased in number and to be extended in scope as was recommended several years ago by Sir George Newman (Chief Medical Officer of the Ministry of Health 1919–35) to cover all the stages of a woman's life and all her ailments. Greatly as she needs the best advice and treatment while she is engaged in bearing and nursing the child, this function combined with the arduousness of her daily life leaves conditions which persist long after she has ceased to receive the treatment that the specialised maternity centre can give. There should, therefore, be centres easily accessible to every woman, to which she could go at any time for advice and treatment on any topic connected with her health, including gynæcological ailments, psychological troubles, the spacing of her family, sterility and so on. A very special relationship of intimacy and confidence can be established between a skilled medical adviser and a woman who has once made up her mind to submit these particular troubles to an expert. Without any morbid emphasis of difficulties, the woman can be given the means and knowledge to keep herself healthy in body and mind and, as far as possible, to adjust herself physically and mentally to the problems of her life. A few such centres already exist and have proved beyond all doubt the wide value of their work in the general domestic happiness and well-being of their patients.

A further extension is needed even of the present maternity services. There are still many women who do not take advantage as they might of the Ante-natal Clinics, particularly with their first child. And a far larger proportion fail to receive post-natal examination and treatment. The official figures for England and Wales for 1937 show that although 54% of all notified births had been seen in ante-natal clinics before delivery, only 10% had attended Post-natal Clinics. In some cases, this is most certainly due to ignorance of existing facilities on the mother's part, but mostly it is due to lack of facilities. London teaching hospitals make it a rule that their maternity patients return four or five weeks after the baby's birth for routine post-natal examination. In this way, post-natal conditions which might otherwise be persistent and have a progressively debilitating effect on the mother's health are arrested at the outset. Similar facilities should be made widely available by every local Health Authority, either as part of the maternity centres or in the closest possible association with clinics or hospitals, municipal or voluntary.

Although Maternity Clinics extended in this way and the Women's Welfare Clinics described above should cover most of the health needs of the woman living in cities and large towns, other schemes will have to be devised for the country woman. In her case, the district nurse appears to fill the role of maternity clinic more than anyone else. It seems desirable to develop this service into a free consultative one available to all country women at all times. At the same time there should be far greater facilities for transport to centres for specialised treatment such as dental treatment. There should be a system of travelling clinics staffed by a doctor and carrying all the necessary equipment for advice on and treatment of those ailments which cannot be dealt with by a nurse, and which are not serious enough to require in-patient hospital treatment.

(b) *The National Health Insurance* system should be extended to cover the wives and dependent children of insured men. This would give the mother the option of consulting an individual doctor of her own choice, if she preferred to do so rather than to attend a hospital or clinic.

(c) *Facilities for Recreation and Holidays.* Health, however, does not depend only on adequate facilities for dealing with sickness or the knowledge of the rudiments of hygiene and dietetics. The balance of work with play, breadth of interest and change of scene are almost equally important for physical well-being as these, and of vital importance to happiness and the development of personality. Both young and middle-aged women need some form of recreation; they need opportunities to use the leisure they may have, and to indulge interests outside their homes. They need to meet their fellows, to form social ties, to talk and laugh, and to eat food that they have not cooked themselves. In short they need a club to which they can go at any time on any day for a few hours' rest and recreation. The club should as far as possible be managed by the members, who should accept responsibility for its success and make plans for its activities. It should be very nearly, if not quite, self-supporting, after the capital expenditure has been met.

How far such a club should combine the facilities for certain of the medical services needed, is a question which need not be discussed here. It should certainly offer classes and talks on health matters, and possibly there should be a general medical department under the care of a woman doctor who would be ready to give general medical advice, without treatment.

Such organisations as the Women's Co-operative Guild, Women's Institutes, women's sections of the political parties, Church socials etc., have done valuable work in this direction. But in the opinion of this Committee they have not gone far enough. They very rarely have premises of their own, and if they have, these are only open for very restricted hours, and for very specialised purposes. They are never able to offer the accommodation or the time for the real relaxation and ease of which every working-mother is in need, for relief from the arduousness and cramped conditions of her work in the home.

Every mother should get a fortnight's holiday away from her home once a year. It is possible that the organisation of these might be in the hands of the clubs. The fact that the mother had made friends there would give the club the opportunity of arranging a holiday, and with the companions, of the woman's own choosing. It should not be difficult to organise a scheme of country holiday homes which would be run to a certain extent on a system of exchange between town and country women.

It is essential that while the mother is away, her home should be in the care of someone she knows and trusts, so that she can rest peacefully assured that any members of the family left at home shall be adequately cared for. If she has no available friend, (and the clubs would make these comparatively easy to find) "home-helps", such as are now found by the maternity services should be available. They could be provided by the medical services or by the Clubs, and they should be available for any occasion on which the woman is away from home or unable to do her own work, such as when she is ill, or when the illness of another member of the family demands her whole attention.

(d) *Food*. Up to the present the policy of agricultural subsidies, marketing boards etc. has been in the interest of the producer and in the nature of emergency measures to save the particular industry from collapse. But instead of makeshift methods of dealing with the serious decline of the industry, agriculture should be developed in close relation to other national interests, especially health. Increased consumption of protective foods would result not only in the elimination of a great deal of ill-health, but in better returns for the producer. It has for instance been calculated that if the consumption of milk were raised to the optimum required by good health, the industry would need two and a half million more cows.

Any assistance given to agriculture should therefore be concentrated on the protective food-stuffs. If the home production and distribution of such foods are stimulated in the right way, encouraging the import of those foods which are produced more cheaply abroad, these foods will be within the purchasing power of the people who need them most, and agriculture will be revived at the same time without any additional cost to the nation.

It is clear that were family incomes increased by Family Allowances or other means, agriculture as well as the building and clothing industries would immediately benefit by the increased purchasing power of a large section of the community. At present milk and other equally essential foods are not only too expensive for the average working-class purse, but are actually often unobtainable. In the country the effect of the Milk Marketing Board has often been that people who live at the gate-way of a milk-producing farm cannot buy milk, because it has not been worth while to the farmer to take out a retailer's licence, and he is not even allowed to sell skim milk which has many of the protective qualities.

III. *Ignorance*

All young women need to educate and equip themselves for the very arduous and skilled job they undertake in marriage and in rearing a family. For most trades and professions years of study and practice are necessary for efficiency but in the most important work of all, that of motherhood, the realisation is only just beginning to dawn that trained knowledge must supplement the woman's instinct. In these days the factory has to a large extent replaced the labour of the housewife in the production of many of the necessities of the home, for instance clothes and certain articles of food. In the same way, ready facilities for her to seek expert advice for herself and her family will, in some measure, make it unnecessary for her to include in her maternal equipment many of the homely arts and sciences in which the nineteenth century mother was often highly skilled. But the standard of fitness is rising steadily, and it must be remembered that even fifty years ago medical science was elementary compared to what it is to-day, especially in the realm of maternity, the care (physical and psychological) of children, dietetics and the principles of nutrition. Infant mortality was extremely high, and motherhood being a natural process which just happened, did not seem to call for any particular attention. So that although it may not now be desirable for mothers to know how to set a broken limb, or to sew up a wound with the needle and cotton out of their work basket, or to brew their own most elaborate "simples" against "mother-fits" or scurvy or the King's Evil or what-not, there is now a whole range of new knowledge largely prophylactic (the most valuable of all) which should be part of the elementary provision of every house-wife for the maintenance of the health and happiness of herself and her family. Mothers are not born—they are made; at present generally at the cost of painful, sometimes tragic, often wasteful experience, completed only when it is too late for them to get another chance.

A beginning has been made in the education of the mother by teaching the school-girl the first principles of cooking and housecraft. It is, however, rare for a girl of 13 or 14 to regard the business of marriage, if she thinks about it at all, as a responsibility demanding specialised knowledge and training. When she has arrived at the age at which she actively looks forward to having her own home and family, a greater response to such training can be aroused. The simple rules for her own physical fitness can and should be taught at school, based on sound knowledge of elementary physiology coupled with fitness exercises and outdoor games and occupations. The post-school period is the one, however, to be seriously tackled, so that in the first place the girl can retain the standard of physical well-being to which she has probably been brought during her school years. It has often been remarked how rapidly the physique of adolescents deteriorates when once they leave the comparatively healthy atmosphere and occupations of school. There should be a period of compulsory attendance at continuation classes, and every effort should be made in these and in the social clubs to which at this time a girl can belong to stimulate a healthy interest in domestic matters, investing them with that aura of science and skill which will give them value in her eyes (and in the eyes of her future husband) and arouse pride in her own proficiency. She should be able if she wishes to carry this training through to a high level of expertness, though for obvious reasons if she is compelled to be working at a wage-earning job at the same time, her time will be limited. But facilities for some training in the care of children should be easily available.

If this training were wisely planned, the young married woman would probably be prepared to continue such classes during at least the first year of marriage, when, unless she has kept on her own wage-earning job, she will be able to give more time and thought to the matter, and will naturally be more interested. At this period she will take an interest in the care of children, in their education and up-bringing. The practical problems of running her own home, probably for the first time, the status of marriage, the responsibilities of the future can all be exploited to great advantage for herself and her family. Local Authorities should be urged to supply such training both in day and evening classes and in welfare centres. Clubs, (such as have been advocated earlier in this chapter,) will arouse the interest of their members in all sorts of problems, social, domestic and political, and these women at least will eagerly avail themselves of these facilities to acquire a high standard of efficiency in their homes; and the unhappy state of apathy which is too often the protective armour of the worn-out middle-aged housewife of to-day, will be a rare phenomenon in the future.

These then are the recommendations which the Women's Health Enquiry Committee confidently put forward as practical remedies for the unhappy state of affairs shown in the investigation of these 1,250 families. There does not appear to the Committee to be anything revolutionary, visionary, extravagant or socially unsound about them. Family life will be strengthened by the increased self-respect which such reforms should bring to the mother. That the country is rich enough to pay for these improvements, even the most expensive of them, cannot be denied. Indeed they are based upon the soundest economy, for it is certain that one of the earliest results of so great an increase in well-being and happiness as they would bring, would be an incalculable saving of expenditure in the cure of disease and the tinkering with destitution. The Committee are confident also of the political soundness of such reforms. Whatever social and economic changes the future may bring, the principle of democratic development of individual happiness and welfare through communal services offered to every citizen, will always be an integral part of wise government.

It is realised that these recommendations only go part of the way towards the planning of the ideal democratic state; but it is hoped that at least they will turn the tide of human erosion where it flows strongest and deepest, by giving freedom and honour to those who perform the most indispensable labour of the world.

SUMMARY OF RECOMMENDATIONS

THE three main causes of the married working woman's difficulties are poverty, ill-health and ignorance.

1. To mitigate Poverty, we recommend:—

   a. The raising of wages by an extension of the machinery of Trades Boards and of collective bargaining.
   b. Increased communal provision for children by:—
      i. An extension of the social services affecting children.
      ii. A system of Family Allowances paid to the mother.[1]
   c. The provision of appropriate subsidies for housing such as eventually to make it possible for every family to have a healthy home at a rent which it can afford.

2. To mitigate Ill-health, we recommend:—

   a. The development and improvement of the existing maternal health services of Local Authorities, and the establishment of gynæcological clinics to deal with all aspects of a woman's physical and psychological life.
   b. The extension of the National Health Insurance system to cover the wives and dependent children of insured men.
   c. The establishment of women's clubs for recreation, holidays and leisure.
   d. The concentration of agricultural subsidies, if any, on protective food-stuffs, so as to bring these within the means of every working-class home.

[1] Miss Tuckwell writes:—I find myself unable to subscribe to 1.b.ii. I have never felt clear that family allowances would not adversely affect the raising of wages which is advocated in 1.a. In any case, I should not be prepared to advocate any proposal which had not the agreed support of the workers whom it would affect, which this proposal so far has not achieved.

3. To mitigate Ignorance, we recommend that increased facilities both in Welfare Centres and through Local Education Authorities should be given to young women, especially to those about to marry or who have been recently married, in the care of the home and of the health and hygiene of the family.

APPENDICES

1. List of places from which information has been drawn.
2. Age in relation to health.
3. Number of pregnancies in relation to health.
4. Incidence of special ailments in relation to housing conditions, pregnancies and income.
5. Income in relation to health.

1. LIST OF PLACES FROM WHICH INFORMATION DRAWN

Places	No. of Cases
Accrington	18
Arbroath	2
Birmingham	246
Blackburn	3
Bolton	9
Brighton	2
Bucks	3
Caerphilly	21
Cardiff	20
Chesterfield	2
Coventry	9
Croydon	73
Derby	39
Devon	32
Durham	24
East Sussex	26
Edinburgh	10
Essex	87
Glasgow	102
Gloucestershire	3
Herts	2
Heston and Isleworth	11
Kent	2
Leeds	7
Liverpool	8
Llanelly	15
London	210
Manchester	7
Newcastle	25
Norfolk	5
Northumberland	4

Places					No. of Cases
Preston	.	.	.	.	.	2
Rhondda	.	.	.	.	.	8
Rochdale	.	.	.	.	.	42
Rotherham	.	.	.	.	.	72
Scarborough	.	.	.	.	.	2
Sheffield	.	.	.	.	.	7
Smethwick	.	.	.	.	.	3
Stafford	.	.	.	.	.	4
Surrey	.	.	.	.	.	24
Woolwich	.	.	.	.	.	59
				Total	1250

2. AGE AND HEALTH

Age in Years	Apparently Good Health	Indifferent Health	Poor Health	Very Bad Health	Total of age Groups
20–29	138	87	35	66	326
30–39	183	137	104	174	598
40–49	62	40	41	111	254
50	9	14	10	39	72
Total of Health Groups	392	278	190	390	1250

3. NUMBER OF PREGNANCIES AND HEALTH

N.B. It is clear that the number of pregnancies is never overstated. Live births are generally (but not always) correctly counted, but miscarriages and even still births are easily forgotten by the women. It is noticed that the woman often corrects herself in the answers she makes to the questions of miscarriages and still births. These figures therefore should, in all probability be higher.

No. of Pregnancies	HEALTH Apparently Good	Indifferent	Bad	Very Bad	TOTALS Of Persons	Of Pregnancies
0	10	3	2	10	25	0
1	87	44	15	28	174	174
2	58	53	28	35	174	348
3	79	43	39	54	215	645
4	45	34	24	43	146	584
5	31	23	.14	48	116	580
6	23	14	26	36	99	594
7	18	18	14	30	80	560
8	11	16	9	30	66	528
9	13	6	7	20	46	414
10	7	9	3	19	38	380
11	5	3	3	10	21	231
12	2	4	1	8	15	180
13	2	5	2	7	16	208
14	1	1	1	8	11	154
15	—	1	—	2	3	45
16	—	1	1	1	3	48
21	—	—	1	—	1	21
22	—	—	—	1	1	22
Total	392	278	190	390	1250	5716

Average numbers of pregnancies (to the nearest single decimal).

4·6 for the whole
3·6 for the good health group
5·6 for the very bad health group

4. INCIDENCE OF SPECIAL AILMENTS RELATIVE TO HOUSING, PREGNANCIES, and INCOME COMPARED WITH THE WHOLE NUMBER AND THE GOOD HEALTH GROUP[1]

N.B. This table is for *comparison only*. As stated in the text it is probable that the incidence of ill-health is understated by the women (certain ailments such as bad teeth, of which a woman can be unaware, more often than others). The figures therefore of each ailment indicate *only* a rough relationship between their incidence and conditions of life.

	Whole Number 1,250	Apparently Good Health Group 392	Anaemia 558	Carious Teeth 165	Constipation 273	Gynaecological 191	Headaches 291	Rheumatism 198	Bad Legs 101
Percentage in bad houses (second and third groups: see chapter on Housing)	31	25·5	70	67	70	66	69	70	66
Average number of pregnancies	4·6	3·6	5·6	5	5	5·2	4·8	5·9	6·5
"Housekeeping" per head per week Percentage with 4/- and under	17·5	10·5	34·6	18	14	18·3	20·2	13·1	25
Percentage with 4/1—6/-	32·5	24	41	52	35·3	40	38	35·3	32
Percentage with 6/1—8/-	20	25·5	17	18·8	25·6	15·2	23·3	23·2	16
Percentage with 8/1—10/-	11·5	14	4·9	7	10·1	14	13	11·2	11
Percentage with 10/- and over	18·5	26	2·5	4·2	15	12·5	5·5	17·2	16

[1] Figures are given to the nearest single decimal

5. HEALTH AND INCOME

220 or about 17·5% with 4/– and under per head per week housekeeping money — of these about —

18% make no complaints about health
16% have indifferent health
20% have poor health
46% have very bad health

406 or about 32·5% with 4/1—6/– per head per week housekeeping money — of these about —

23% make no complaints about health
12% have indifferent health
15% have poor health
50% have very bad health

250 or about 20% with 6/1—8/– per head per week housekeeping money — of these about —

40% make no complaints about health
20% have indifferent health
15% have poor health
25% have very bad health

144 or about 11·5% with 8/1—10/– per head per week housekeeping money — of these about —

38% make no complaints about health
33% have indifferent health
9% have poor health
20% have very bad health

230 or about 18·5% with over 10/– per head per week housekeeping money — of these about —

43% make no complaints about health
26% have indifferent health
14% have poor health
17% have very bad health

N.B. Decimal points in the distribution of health in each income group have been omitted.